D0891532

Beyond the Theme Parks: Exploring Central Florida

Beyond the Theme Parks

❋ Exploring Central Florida

Benjamin D. Brotemarkle

University Press of Florida

Gainesville · Tallahassee · Tampa · Boca Raton

Pensacola · Orlando · Miami · Jacksonville

115251

Copyright 1999 by the Board of Regents of the State of Florida
Printed in the United States of America on acid-free paper ∞
All rights reserved

04   03   02   01   00   99   6   5   4   3   2   1

All photographs in this volume are by Benjamin Brotemarkle.

Library of Congress Cataloging-in-Publication Data
Brotemarkle, Benjamin D.
Beyond the theme parks: exploring central Florida / Benjamin
Brotemarkle.
p. cm.
Includes bibliographical references and index.
ISBN 0-8130-1657-6 (alk. paper)
1. Florida—Guidebooks. I. Title.
F309.3.B76   1999
917.5904'63—dc21   98-46870

The University Press of Florida is the scholarly publishing agency for
the State University System of Florida, comprising Florida A & M
University, Florida Atlantic University, Florida International University,
Florida State University, University of Central Florida, University of
Florida, University of North Florida, University of South Florida, and
University of West Florida.

University Press of Florida
15 Northwest 15th Street
Gainesville, FL 32611
http://nersp.nerdc.ufl.edu/~upf

To my nephews Alex and Ben Turner
with the hope that they grow up with an
appreciation for their cultural heritage

Contents

Illustrations

Preface

Contrary to popular belief, there is much more to life in Central Florida than theme parks, basketball, and beaches. The region has a long and colorful history that enriches the present and paves the way for the future. This book examines historic preservation efforts and active cultural celebrations that commemorate Central Florida's past, providing residents with a sense of community and visitors with interesting options to augment a theme park vacation.

As producer and host of the weekly public radio program *The Arts Connection*, heard throughout Central Florida on 90.7 WMFE-FM, I have had the opportunity to interview many people at the forefront of historic and cultural preservation in this area. These interviews, conducted between January 1990 and July 1997, are the source for much of the information contained in this book.

The Arts Connection is annually funded by a Special Project Grant from United Arts of Central Florida and by the Florida Department of State, Division of Cultural Affairs. The show has been awarded many local, state, and regional journalism awards. My work has also been heard around the world on Voice of America Radio, across the country on National Public Radio, and throughout the state on Florida Public Radio. I also have the opportunity periodically to produce and host public television specials looking at local history and culture.

My interest in historic and cultural preservation has also been fueled by my college experience. I earned a master of liberal studies degree and a bachelor of arts degree in humanities from Rollins College. I also have an associate degree in voice performance from the Florida School of the Arts at St. Johns River Community College, which has enabled me to perform in dozens of Orlando Opera Company productions, with Seaside Music Theater in Daytona Beach, and in *Cross and Sword* (the official state play of Florida) in St. Augustine.

This book began as an independent study project that would count as an elective credit toward my master of liberal studies degree, but it soon acquired a life of its own. After many additions and revisions, the project became my final thesis. I owe a debt of gratitude to Barry Levis, professor of history at Rollins College, and Ed Cohen, director of the master of liberal studies program, for serving as my mentors during the writing process.

I also wish to thank the many people who are quoted in this book and give it substance. In particular I thank N.Y. Nathiri, executive director of the Association to Preserve the Eatonville Community and founder of the Zora Neale Hurston Festival of the Arts and Humanities. Mrs. Nathiri's work is an inspiration to me personally and a model for anyone hoping to encourage a sense of community in the present by celebrating the past.

I could not have written this book without the hours and hours of interviews that I have accumulated as producer of The Arts Connection. I thank all the people who have made my career in public radio possible, including Stephen McKenney Steck, Dale Spear, Robert Peterson, Cynthia Link, and Jose Fajardo. I also thank all the people who have contributed their efforts to the program over the years, including Jackie Brockington, Dave Pignanelli, Rick Andrews, Kevin Nissley, Gavin Sutton, Dave Glerum, Michael Vonderbrink, Chris Howell, Amy Fegebank, Wendy McCabe, Pat Duggins, Lakshmi Singh, Doris Keeler, Gail Ryan, Bernadine Clark, Kristen Ludecke, J. Stephen Brooks, and Barbra McIntyre.

Thanks also to my father, David Brotemarkle, and my mother, true crime author Anna Flowers, for their encouragement and support. Thanks to my sister Belle Turner, to writer Carol Jose, and to Michelle Alexander and Sara Van Arsdel from the Orange County Historical Society for their helpful suggestions. Thanks to my sister-in-law Vicki Candiotti, whose computer troubleshooting skills saved large portions of this book from disappearing before my eyes. Thanks also to Clare and Brian Martin, Faye Rudd, Irene Becker, and the rest of my family and friends for their interest in this project.

My biggest thanks go to my wonderful wife, Christina, for her love, patience, understanding, and constructive criticism.

I believe strongly in the need for historic and cultural preservation in Central Florida, for both residents and visitors, and I hope that this book will stimulate an interest in celebrating our past.

Beyond the Theme Parks: Exploring Central Florida

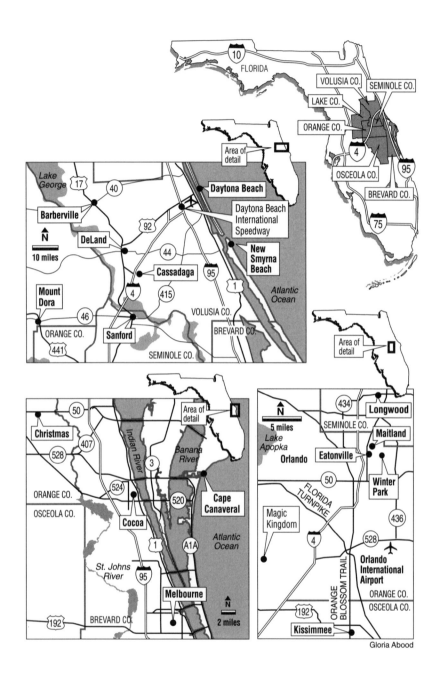

Gloria Abood

Introduction

Central Florida is recognized as the home of Disney World and other theme parks, the residence of the Orlando Magic basketball team, and the launch site of America's explorations in space. Many of the people living in the region, along with most of the tourists who come to the area, share this quite limited view of Central Florida. Some tourists never venture beyond Disney property once they arrive at their hotel rooms, missing out on a wide range of available cultural activities. Even more lamentable is the fact that residents of Central Florida are often unaware of the area's rich cultural heritage.

People both visiting and living in Central Florida complain that the area has no sense of community, that it has a superficial culture, and that the region has shallow historical roots. Many people who have lived in Central Florida for more than a decade, establishing successful careers and raising families here, still think of somewhere else as home.

This book serves three purposes. First, it can be used by visitors to Central Florida as a guide to a wide range of interesting historical sites and exciting cultural activities that will augment any vacation in the area. Second, the tens of thousands of people who move to the area every year can use the information presented here to acquire an appreciation for and understanding of the culture of their new home. Finally, this study of Central Florida will offer people already living in the area a sense of community by introducing them to active celebrations of cultural heritage in which they can participate.

It may also be helpful to examine what this book is not intended to be. Although it explores much of the history of the region, this work does not serve as a complete history of Central Florida. Similarly, although we visit many cultural events and discuss the activities of many of the area's arts institutions, a complete survey of local arts groups is found only in appendix A. We go to many Central Florida towns but do not examine every community on the map. Historic buildings are discussed, but a complete listing of historic sites in the region is found only in appendix B. This book focuses on historic preservation efforts and active cultural celebrations that, through a tie to Central Florida's past, can help to promote a sense of community in the present and future.

Before proceeding with this endeavor, we must establish a further definition of our boundaries. Geographically, Central Florida includes the entire portion of the state from just south of Gainesville to just north of Lake Okeechobee. Much of this geographic area, however, is commonly labeled North Florida, South Florida, and the Gulf Coast. Most people looking at a map would place Tampa in Central Florida, but that city is the home of the University of South Florida. Although it may seem to be arbitrary, the region referred to as Central Florida is generally limited to Orange, Seminole, Osceola, Lake, Volusia, and Brevard Counties. This book adheres to that popular usage.

As of 1994, census reports indicate that 1,187,833 people live in the greater metropolitan Orlando area, which includes Orange, Seminole, and Osceola Counties. While some of this population is transient, tens of thousands of additional people move here every year. The Orlando Chamber of Commerce says that 33,961,000 people visited the Orlando area in 1994, making it "the world's most popular vacation destination." According to the Daytona Beach Area Visitors and Convention Bureau, 8,000,000 people visit that portion of Central Florida every year, joining Daytona's 78,000 permanent residents. The population of Brevard County is estimated to be 435,000; Lake County's population is listed as 171,168; and hundreds of thousands of people visit both of those counties each year. Unfortunately, many of the people who visit and live in Central Florida are unaware of the area's diverse cultural heritage.

Historic preservation and the active celebration of culture provide a sense of community. The Zora Neale Hurston Festival of the Arts and Humanities, which we will visit on pages 35–46, stands alone as the best example of how Central Floridians can exploit history in a positive way to strengthen their communities. Poet and performing artist Maya Angelou praises the Hurston Festival's mission of preserving African American culture, and emphasized to me in an interview that remembering the past is essential: "All people need to know their heritage. A person who doesn't know where he's been has little chance of charting where he or she is going. I do believe that people live in direct relation to the heroes and she-roes they have, always and in all ways. All those people who went before and paid for you, Mr. Brotemarkle, and for me, need to be cherished. Just the grace of saying 'thank you' increases and enriches our present lives, and prepares us to enrich the lives of those who are yet to come."[1] While traveling through Central Florida in this book, we will see how history promotes solidarity in the present and hope for the future.

Although it is unfortunate that Central Florida is known primarily for theme parks and basketball, it should be stated here that this work is in no way meant to disparage either Walt Disney World and its affiliated theme parks or the Orlando Magic basketball team. The Disney Corporation has contributed greatly to the culture of Central Florida by financially supporting area arts and cultural organizations, by supporting arts education efforts, and by building an amphitheater in Lake Eola Park in downtown Orlando, which is used by the Orlando Shakespeare Festival and other groups. While Disney does not release employment statistics, it is estimated that the company employs more than 50,000 Central Floridians.

The Walt Disney Amphitheater at Lake Eola Park in downtown Orlando is the venue for the Orlando-UCF Shakespeare Festival and a variety of other cultural celebrations. Disney also hosts the annual Festival of the Masters outdoor art show, stimulates the local film industry, and brings important performing artists to the area.

Similarly, the Orlando Magic basketball team has helped the economy of Central Florida, and both the team and its individual members have donated time and money to a variety of important projects, such as efforts to keep local youth from using drugs. When the Magic won the National Basketball Association Eastern Conference Championship in 1995, it galvanized the Central Florida community like no other cultural phenomenon. Orlando Magic T-shirts, signs, and banners were visible everywhere in the region, both during and after the championship games. Widespread public support for the team continues today. Many people who previously had no interest in professional basketball have been absorbed into the frenzy surrounding the Magic, which demonstrates the hunger of Central Floridians for something that will give them a sense of community. Learning about the living history of the region can also engender community bonding.

The presence of active arts and cultural institutions can also help to promote a sense of community. The demise of the Florida Symphony Orchestra perpetuates the popular misconception of Central Florida as a cultural

The Orlando Arena is the home of the Orlando Magic basketball team, the Solar Bears hockey team, and the Orlando Predators arena football team; it also hosts other indoor sporting events. The "Orena" is also the venue for popular music concerts and large touring productions such as *Lord of the Dance*. The adjacent Bob Carr Performing Arts Center is the venue for national touring productions of Broadway shows, classical music concerts, Orlando Opera Company performances, and Southern Ballet Theater presentations.

wasteland. In the spring of 1994, the FSO was forced to cease operation because of financial difficulties. Some people blame the orchestra musicians' strike of 1990 for creating a feeling of ill will between the FSO and symphony patrons, but in its last years of existence, orchestra members, management, and the community were working together to save the symphony. Others point to bad management as the reason for the failure of the FSO, but a new executive director and new members of the board of directors had created a reasonable and viable business plan for the orchestra, which they never had an opportunity to implement. Still others blame the city and local government for not securing a loan of four hundred thousand dollars for the orchestra to keep it in business long enough to generate more income through newly planned regional concerts. Whatever the reason, like many other cities across the country, Orlando lost what had been the cornerstone of its cultural community.

Although the loss of the Florida Symphony Orchestra should not be minimized, Central Florida nevertheless maintains a strong and active arts and cultural community. United Arts of Central Florida, an umbrella fundraising organization, has allowed the area's major arts and cultural institutions to thrive. United Arts provides funds for smaller arts groups and individual artists through Special Project Grants.

Central Florida's major cultural institutions provide visitors and residents with a wide variety of entertaining and educational programs. The Orlando Opera Company has been producing a full season since the 1960s, featuring operatic greats such as Roberta Peters, Sherrill Milnes, Luciano Pavarotti, and Cecilia Bartoli, as well as local singing actors. Civic Theater of Central Florida offers classes in theater arts to both children and adults and provides a variety of theatrical experiences throughout the year on three separate stages. Southern Ballet Theater presents newly developed experimental dance pieces, as well as traditional dance favorites.

The Orlando Museum of Art completed a $13-million renovation and expansion in early 1997 that has doubled the size of the museum. The improvements are allowing the museum to display more of its expansive permanent collection of works and to bring stimulating traveling exhibitions such as "The Imperial Tombs of China" to the area.

Marena Grant Morrisey, executive director of the Orlando Museum of

Art, believes that the museum is now in a position to have a significant impact on the economy of Central Florida by stimulating cultural tourism: "When the Orlando Museum of Art announced its strategic plan to present world-class exhibitions, we received a tremendous response from the Convention and Tourism Bureau and the Economic Development Commission because they saw the educational and cultural component of Orlando as something that could add to cultural tourism. Our plans, plus the plans of the Science Center and eventually the Historical Museum, to reach a whole new level of excellence in programming, culturally and educationally, were of great interest to them. Absolutely these plans will play a great part in the economic development of our area. In fact, they are projecting just from 'The Imperial Tombs of China' that our local community will benefit between $58 million and $137 million in new money because of people coming to this show and staying here, spending money throughout our community."[2]

Many smaller arts groups are active in Central Florida. The Orlando Theater Project and Theater Downtown both produce exciting seasons of dramatic presentations. The annual Orlando International Fringe Festival, held in April, brings ten days of alternative theater, music, and performance art to downtown Orlando. Dozens of other theaters, art galleries, and musical

The Orlando Museum of Art, expanded and renovated in 1997, has an extensive permanent collection of works from the past several centuries, as well as African and pre-Columbian art. The museum also hosts blockbuster touring exhibitions such as "The Imperial Tombs of China" and "A Century of Masterworks: Selections from the Edward R. Broida Collection."

groups provide an outlet for local artists. Organizations like the Asian Cultural Association and events like the Scottish Highland Games celebrate the area's ethnic diversity. Although these groups and festivals enrich the cultural climate of Central Florida, this work will concentrate on those organizations and events that are directly related to the history of the region.

Orlando Mayor Glenda Hood, a supporter of the arts, serves as a primary fund-raiser for United Arts of Central Florida and leads efforts to build a new performing arts complex in the city. Mayor Hood also realizes that historic preservation has practical benefits as well as aesthetic value, contributing to community pride and stimulating tourism: "Historic preservation is extremely important. The only way that we can plan for the future in the right way is to understand the past, and being able to have that historical perspective allows our young people to learn better and grow stronger. Orlando has been a leader in historic preservation with individual homes and buildings and facilities, with neighborhoods, and a number of historic districts that have been put in place. I think you're going to see more and more people realize that a community, yes, needs to be progressive and look to the future, but they need to learn from the past."[3]

Unfortunately, many Central Floridians are apparently more interested in developing Orlando as a major city of the future than in celebrating its indigenous cultural heritage. Many historic hotels and other buildings in Orlando have been destroyed in the name of progress, and a lasting event recognizing the history of the city has yet to be established. Perhaps this book can help to stimulate an interest in cultural preservation among the residents of Orlando and its surrounding communities.

The physical preservation of historic buildings and the establishment of high-quality cultural festivals could be the key to the future growth of the Orlando area. Central Florida is in a unique position to reap the economic benefits of the increasing interest in cultural and heritage tourism. According to statistics gathered by the Travel Industry Association of America, 54 million Americans took at least one trip in 1996 of one hundred miles or more that included a visit to a museum or historic site. Additionally, 33 million Americans took a trip specifically to visit a cultural event or festival.

With more than 40 million people visiting Central Florida every year, the potential economic impact of cultural and heritage tourism on the area is significant, a fact not lost on political leaders. In 1997, the Florida Commission on Tourism created the Ecotourism/Heritage Tourism Advisory Committee. Florida Governor Lawton Chiles appointed the committee to develop a state-wide regionally based plan to promote the historical and cultural assets of the state, as well as its natural attributes.

The Ecotourism/Heritage Tourism Advisory Committee defines *heritage* as "evidence of our history and culture. It is represented in our customs, values and beliefs, as well as the material expressions and products of these ways of behaving. It is our inheritance as a society, and gives us a sense of who we are." In coming years the committee will work with the Florida State Legislature to establish and promote vacation opportunities that include "festivals and events that reflect the richness and diversity of our past, museums and other interpretive facilities that collect and display evidence of our history and culture in its many aspects."[4]

Sara Van Arsdel, executive director of the Orange County Historical Museum, is one of Central Florida's leading historic preservationists. While Van Arsdel is optimistic about the growing interest in local historic preservation, she is concerned that not enough is being done to protect Central Florida's rich cultural heritage: "Being an historian and being someone who champions this, I really want to see more efforts done. I think we have an uphill battle. A lot of people in this community don't realize the history that is here B.D.—before Disney. I think that they would have a much stronger identity with the community, and with community efforts going on, if they knew and appreciated local history and its importance in their lives. I think that as people become more aware and more sensitive, and as we're going into another century, it gives us time to pause, to think about things that have happened in the twentieth century, particularly the early twentieth century."[5]

This book is intended to increase awareness of Central Florida history and culture among its inhabitants and visitors, and inspire an active interest in historic preservation. We begin our journey through the cultural heritage of Central Florida in Orange County and progress outward to the other areas of the region in a rough spiral. After visiting Seminole County, we will travel down to Osceola County, over to Lake County, up into Volusia County, then back down to Brevard County.

❊ Orlando

More than the Magic Kingdom

A corporate jet soaring across the Central Florida sky in early 1965 was carrying cartoonist, filmmaker, and visionary entrepreneur Walt Disney. Inspired by the huge success of the theme park Disneyland in Anaheim, California, Disney wanted to develop his original idea more fully by creating an expansive family vacation destination on America's east coast. Attracted by Florida's temperate climate and already established tourist trade, Disney decided to build his new "Magic Kingdom" in the center of the state, near Orlando.[1]

As Disney's jet flew just south of Orlando, he noticed that, with the exception of some orange groves, the land surrounding the intersection of the Florida Turnpike and the just-completed Interstate 4 was virtually undeveloped. Disney decided this would be the perfect spot for his new entertainment mecca since the highways would provide easy access, and the undeveloped countryside would allow almost endless expansion.[2]

Very quietly, Disney acquired almost forty-three square miles of Central Florida land by October 1965. Nearby residents speculated wildly that a huge industrial plant or some secret government installation was being built in their backyard.[3] The following month Disney held a press conference in Orlando announcing his plans to develop Walt Disney World, a much larger version of Disneyland that (unlike the California park) had room for further expansion. Also explained were plans for

the Experimental Prototype Community of Tomorrow (EPCOT), a city celebrating world culture, where research to benefit humankind would take
place.[4]

Walt Disney died in December 1966, before seeing his vision for Central
Florida realized. Walt Disney World opened in October 1971 at a cost of
$400 million. The success of the theme park attracted others such as Sea
World of Florida and Universal Studios Florida.[5]

EPCOT was built soon after Disney World was completed. The theme
park is not the self-contained community that Walt Disney had planned,
but it does celebrate scientific accomplishments and world culture through
entertaining rides and exhibits.[6] Construction on Disney property continued with Disney-MGM Studios. While the park essentially focuses on the
products of the Disney-MGM film company through rides, parades, and
restaurants, some television and movie production does take place there.
Downtown Disney at Pleasure Island provides nightlife for Disney visitors
with a series of themed bars, specialty stores, and a theater complex.

The Disney Institute offers educational vacation experiences through
informal classes and lectures on subjects such as rock climbing, landscap-
ing, and drawing cartoons. There are many hotels on Disney property, ful-
filling Walt Disney's dream of a self-contained vacation wonderland. Celebration is an independent residential community on Disney property that
strives to promote a small-town atmosphere. Most recently, in the spring of
1998, the Disney corporation opened Animal Kingdom, a theme park designed to replicate an African safari.

Walt Disney World and its neighboring theme parks are undoubtedly
responsible for Orlando's earning the distinction "the world's most popular vacation destination."[7] Tens of millions of people visit Central Florida
every year, primarily to see the home of Mickey Mouse. People who lived in
Orlando prior to the construction of Disney's entertainment empire have
watched their small town grow into a sprawling city with hundreds of
hotels, shopping malls, souvenir shops, and bedroom communities.

While much of the growth in Orlando is caused by Disney World, the city
has a long and colorful history dating back to the 1830s. Orlando currently
has no cultural celebration recognizing its history, but some preservation
efforts are under way that will leave a lasting legacy for future generations.

Many Florida towns, including Orlando, have been built around forts constructed in the 1830s during the Seminole Indian Wars. The United States government strategically placed these forts about a day's walk apart to protect marching groups of soldiers from attacks at night.[8] We will look at the circumstances of the Seminole Indian Wars on pages 57–63, when we visit the replica of Fort Christmas, located just northeast of Orlando.

The site of the fort built in the area that would later become Orlando is now private property. The intersection where Summerlin Avenue dead-ends into Gatlin Avenue in southeast Orlando is currently a residential area and the site of a small naval research lab. A stone marker placed by a private driveway at the intersection reads, "Erected by the Orlando Chapter, D.A.R., March 27, 1924, marking the site of Fort Gatlin, 1838, military outpost."[9] In the summer of 1997, ground-penetrating radar detected what could be the buried remains of Fort Gatlin on the research lab grounds.[10] Prior to the establishment of Fort Gatlin, Native Americans were the only inhabitants of the land that would become Orlando.

The community that arose around Fort Gatlin officially became the city of Orlando in 1875, when the twenty-nine local residents voted to make one square mile of what is now the downtown area their municipality.[11] While it is unknown how the name of the city was selected, there are several interesting theories.

In 1842 a Georgia man named Aaron Jernigan settled his family in Central Florida. The Jernigan family had seven hundred cattle and raised a variety of crops, including sugar cane, sweet potatoes, cotton, and pumpkins. The small community took the name Jernigan in honor of the prosperous family. The first post office in the area was opened in 1850, and the community name was changed to Orlando in 1857.[12] This is where the mystery begins.

A judge from South Carolina, named J. G. Speer, had moved to Florida in 1854 and helped to organize Orange County. In 1856 he was responsible for having the county seat moved from Enterprise to Orlando. Some people believe that Speer named Orlando after the character in Shakespeare's comedy *As You Like It*, because he was a fan of the bard.[13] People who favor this theory point to the fact that one of Orlando's major downtown streets is called Rosalind, the name of another character from the same play.

Another popular legend of how Orlando got its name centers around a man named "Mr. Orlando" who died near the site of Fort Gatlin while taking an ox caravan to Tampa. He was supposedly buried at the spot where he died, and people passing through Central Florida would say, "There lies Orlando."[14]

For many years it was popularly accepted that the city of Orlando was named after a soldier named Orlando Reeves, who was killed by Seminole Indians in 1835. It was believed that Reeves gave his life protecting other soldiers against a sneak attack as they camped outside Fort Gatlin.[15] While generally agreeing with this account of how Orlando was named, a newspaper story from 1884 identifies the name of the soldier who gave his life for his comrades as Orlando Jennings.[16]

During Orlando's centennial celebration in 1975, researchers tried to clear up the controversy. War Department records listing the names of the 1,466 soldiers killed during the Seminole Indian Wars were consulted, but to the researchers' surprise, neither an Orlando Reeves nor an Orlando Jennings was on the roster.[17]

Further research uncovered the fact that a very wealthy plantation owner named Orlando J. Rees lived near Fort Gatlin in the 1830s and was nicknamed "Colonel" Rees, although he had not served in the military. A letter Rees wrote to the U.S. government in 1837 states that he had trouble with the Seminole Indians, who "stole" some of his 110 slaves by offering them a better quality of life and protection. The 1840 census indicates that Rees no longer operated his huge cattle ranch and farm in Central Florida.[18]

The discovery of O. J. Rees raised as many questions as it answered. Was "Colonel" Orlando J. Rees incorrectly identified as the "soldier" Orlando Reeves? Does the middle initial in Rees's name stand for "Jennings," leading to the further confusion over the city of Orlando's namesake? Does the fact that Rees had trouble with the Seminoles indicate that he may have been killed by them? Did Rees simply move away from Central Florida prior to the 1840 census, or was his plantation abandoned following his death? Historians are still trying to answer these questions.

Whatever the circumstances behind the 1857 naming of Orlando, in 1875 the city was incorporated and has experienced several periods of intense growth prior to the opening of Disney World in 1971. Sara Van Arsdel, executive director of the Orange County Historical Society, explains the chronology of Orlando's transformation from a small town into a major city: "The most important first period of growth and development was in the 1880s, when the railroads came in. That opened the area up for great settlement. It also provided a swift means of transportation for the citrus industry, which at that time was just starting out, but it made it easier to get the products to market in a very fast way, and it really opened the area up for development. The next cycle of really great development was in the 1920s. Florida participated in the great land boom. As [did] the rest of Florida, Orlando and Orange County suffered the depression at least four years before the great stock market crash, because the bottom dropped out of the real estate market here, and prices fell, and people were out of work much earlier than the Depression. The next boom period was after World War II. Orlando did participate in the war, and a lot of the things that happened during the war made the way for the development that occurred afterwards. The development of the space program at Cape Canaveral and the decision by Glenn Martin to move Martin Marietta and to establish a plant here in Orlando was a tremendous decision because that led to the development of the infrastructure that is so important today—roads, the Turnpike, I-4—all of that led to the Disney boom."[19]

Another milestone in the history of Orlando is the Big Freeze of 1894–95, which virtually destroyed the area's thriving citrus industry. During that winter the temperatures in Orlando fell to as low as eleven degrees, killing nearly all of the orange trees in the region. The impact that the harsh winter had on Orlando is indicated by the fact that the city's population in 1900 was 2,481, about 500 fewer than the population in 1880.[20] Only the successful tourism trade kept more people from leaving Orlando before the turn of the century.

The presence of military forces in Orlando contributed greatly to the city's growth throughout much of the twentieth century. In 1940 the Army Air Corps established an air base in Orlando, using runways that are now part of the Orlando Executive Airport. The base was the home of the Twenty-third Composite Group.[21] This influx of soldiers added money to the local economy. By 1943 the Orlando air base was the home of the Army Air Force Tactical Air Command (AAFTAC), a school that trained pilots for secret military missions.[22]

Throughout the 1940s and 1950s the Orlando base was used for a variety of purposes. AAFTAC was replaced by the "Fighting Tigers" of the Fourteenth Air Force. In the early 1950s the base was used as an aviation engineers' training school and was then taken over by the Military Air Transport Service. The Orlando Air Force Base also served as the home of the Missile Training Wing of the Tactical Air Command and as the Non-Commissioned Officer Academy. By the mid-1960s budget cutbacks caused the Air Force to close its Orlando base.[23]

In 1968 the Navy took over the former air base and established the Naval Training Center, Orlando. The Navy base and its adjacent hospital pumped millions of dollars into the Central Florida economy for the next two decades. The base and its adjacent hospital employed almost 18,000 military and civilian personnel, and a constant flow of recruits streamed in and out of the base.[24] Navy uniforms were frequently seen at local shopping malls, restaurants, and tourist attractions. In the early 1990s, however, military downsizing once again affected Orlando's military presence. Today only the Navy's Nuclear Power School is still active in Orlando, and the base is virtually deserted.

As the twenty-first century approaches, Orlando's government and civic leaders are working hard to transform what was once a quiet small town into a major world city. In recent years Orlando has acquired major sports teams, built an indoor arena, renovated and expanded its large outdoor stadium, hosted World Cup and Olympic soccer, initiated public transportation projects, enlarged the Orlando International Airport, and encouraged new business activity in the city. Plans to build a major performing arts complex to augment the Bob Carr Auditorium are moving forward.

Some residents who are watching Orlando's rapid growth accuse city leaders of being more concerned with expansion and progress than with preserving the area's historic cultural heritage. The hope for progress and the concern for maintaining the past are beginning to coexist well, however, as city leaders realize that historic preservation can be used as a tool to uplift neighborhoods in economic and social decline and that retaining Orlando's unique character can be useful in attracting new businesses and tourists.

Orlando currently has six designated historic districts: Downtown, Lake Cherokee, Lake Copeland, Lake Eola Heights, Lake Lawsona, and Griffin

Park. Many of Orlando's oldest commercial buildings are in the Downtown Historic District, which consists of several blocks between Church Street and Washington Street. Victorian, Queen Anne, Mediterranean revival, and prairie school homes built between 1875 and 1896 are in the Lake Cherokee Historic District, as well as two Art Deco apartment complexes from the 1940s. The Lake Copeland and Griffin Park Historic Districts are the sites of homes constructed between 1910 and 1940. Homes dating from the mid-1890s are in the Lake Lawsona Historic District.[25]

Other historic buildings in Orlando include the J. J. Bridges House, a colonial revival house on Kuhl Avenue, built in 1916; the Dr. Phillips House on Lake Lucerne, constructed in 1893; the Old Orlando Railroad Depot from 1889 on West Church Street; and the First Church of Christ Scientist from 1926 on Rosalind Avenue. The Rogers Building on South Magnolia Avenue, constructed as a social club for British immigrants, is one of the most distinctive late-nineteenth-century buildings in Florida.[26]

The Harry P. Leu House in Leu Botanical Gardens is on the site of the Mizell family homestead from the 1860s. Several prominent families have lived on the property over the past century. The Leu House was originally built in 1888, but many additions have been made. Originally a typical Florida Cracker house, various residents have added a dining room, rooms for entertaining, bedrooms, and bathrooms. In the 1930s Harry P. Leu planted more than fifteen hundred camellia bushes from China and other exotic plants on the property. Leu donated the fifty-acre site to the city of Orlando in 1961. The Leu Botanical Gardens now hosts chamber music concerts, weddings, and other social events.

The city of Orlando actively maintains many brick roads in downtown neighborhoods and encourages the upkeep of both historic private homes and public buildings. While many important structures have been destroyed to make room for modern multistory buildings, the value of preservation is gradually being realized.

Jodi Rubin, Orlando's historic preservation officer, heads the city's preservation efforts. She explains: "Historic preservation has many roles, but one of them is as an economic revitalization tool for a very small area like a small neighborhood or an intersection or, actually, as it builds, for a whole community, so it's a good revitalization tool. As far as quality of life or choices in life, preserved historic areas are much different than suburbia and suburban strip malls, and those types of things, and [preservation] gives people a choice so that there's not this sameness in a community. The other thing that's happened is that in the downtown area, many of the buildings have been redeveloped for different uses than they were originally intended for. For instance, the Firestone Building, which used to be a tire and service center, is now a nightclub. Some of the other buildings that maybe were stores and offices early on in their histories are now clubs or bars or restaurants or specialty stores. That's the nice thing about preservation: . . . you take a building and kind of fit your new use to that existing building, and still keep the old character of it."[27]

The most obvious example of historic Orlando buildings being redeveloped to serve a new function is the entertainment complex Church Street Station. In 1974 the abandoned Orlando Hotel and the Strand Hotel, both built in the 1920s, were transformed into the bars, restaurants, and shops that make up Church Street Station. As the complex grew, it overtook the Bumby Hardware Store, which was constructed in 1884.[28]

The Bumby Hardware Store, built in 1884, is now a clothing store in the Church Street Station entertainment complex. This complex is also the site of Orlando's first brick train depot, constructed in 1912. Two hotels built in 1920, the Orlando Hotel and the Strand Hotel, have been absorbed by the Church Street Station complex.

Orlando's first brick train depot is at Church Street Station, and a 1912 steam engine has been placed on the railroad tracks that run alongside the Good Time Emporium to add historic ambience.[29] While the Church Street Station development has saved the basic structures of several historic buildings, some have argued that the renovations have been so extensive that the original character of the buildings has been transformed beyond recognition.

Two historic preservation efforts are under way in Orlando that retain a sense of the city's past in function as well as appearance. The construction of a modern high-rise courthouse, completed in 1998, has allowed the courthouse built in 1927, located just a few blocks away, to be transformed into the Orange County Regional History Center, home of the Orange County Historical Society. Exhibitions to be displayed in the old courthouse will celebrate local history.

The Orange County Courthouse, built in 1927, is the twenty-first-century home of the Orange County Regional History Center. Moving into the abandoned courthouse will allow the Orange County Historical Society to present a wide variety of permanent displays. Renovations on the courthouse began in April 1998.

On the other side of the six-lane Interstate 4, the abandoned Wellsbilt Hotel is becoming the Museum of African American History. As Orlando grew rapidly during the land boom of the 1920s, an African American community was established in the southwest section of the city. One of the community's most prominent citizens, Dr. William Wells, constructed the Wellsbilt Hotel and the adjacent South Street Casino. In the days of racial segregation, prior to the civil rights laws of the 1960s, many important African Americans such as former Supreme Court Justice Thurgood Marshall and baseball great Roy Campanella stayed at the Wellsbilt Hotel. Legendary musicians like Ella Fitzgerald, Ray Charles, and Peg Leg Bates temporarily lived in the Wellsbilt Hotel and performed in the South Street Casino next door.[30]

Leading the effort to transform the Wellsbilt Hotel into the Museum of African American History are the Trust for Public Land, the Orlando Magic Youth Foundation, the city of Orlando, and the Association to Preserve African American Society, History, and Tradition (PAST). Geraldine Thompson is president of PAST, a nonprofit organization founded in 1991 to research and document the history and cultural contributions of African Americans in Central Florida. She explains the important role of William Wells: "Dr. Wells was one of the pioneer African American physicians in Orlando, and he delivered probably half of the African American population in Orlando in the fifties and sixties. And not only was he a physician and provided health care to residents here, but he also was concerned about the social life and the cultural life of African Americans in the Central Florida area. He constructed the Wellsbilt Hotel in 1929, and he also constructed the South Street Casino, which was located next door, and was the location of celebrations of graduations, weddings, memorable events in folks' lives, dances, and just a location like community centers are today, for people to gather and commemorate events in their lives. So he really was an outstanding individual in terms of the African American community, and what he gave back to that community."[31]

Following the end of racial segregation in the 1960s, African Americans who came to Orlando could legally stay in any hotel. In the 1970s and 1980s the Wellsbilt Hotel and the South Street Casino were neglected and eventually abandoned. The South Street Casino was torn down in 1987, and until the recent historic preservation efforts began, a long list of building code violations threatened the Wellsbilt Hotel with destruction. PAST President Geraldine Thompson explains that the dispersal of the previously close knit African American community in Orlando also contributed to the demise of the Wellsbilt Hotel: "[There was] a shift of population from the downtown area at the end of segregation. People could live wherever they could afford to live, and so people moved out into the suburbs. It's just like the dominant culture moving out into the suburbs, and so you have more urban sprawl, if you will, in the Orlando area. And so people by and large abandoned the downtown area in terms of residential living. There's been a lot of effort to revitalize downtown on the east side of Division Street, and we're now doing the same thing on the west side of Division."[32]

Plans for the African American museum to be housed in the Wellsbilt Hotel include a continuous series of exhibitions focusing on jazz musicians and other historically significant people. It is hoped that the museum will foster a sense of pride in the black community, particularly among young

The abandoned Wellsbilt Hotel, built in 1929, is being transformed into the Museum of African-American History. Many prominent African Americans, such as Thurgood Marshall and Ella Fitzgerald, stayed at the Wellsbilt Hotel prior to the establishment of civil rights laws in the 1960s. Plans for the museum include displays celebrating jazz musicians and African-American community leaders.

people, and therefore help to fight problems faced by the community, such as crime and drug abuse. The museum will also increase awareness of the important cultural contributions of African Americans among people of other races, encouraging mutual respect and racial harmony in the Central Florida community.

The African American community in Orlando was established long before William Wells built his hotel and casino. The Reverend Andrew Hooper, a white man, built homes for African Americans in 1886. The west Orlando community was named the Callahan neighborhood in 1947 to honor the black physician Jerry B. Callahan. When Jones High School opened on Parramore Avenue in 1921, it joined Eatonville's Hungerford School as one of the only black educational institutions in Central Florida. Jones High School is now the Callahan Neighborhood Center.[33]

Other historic buildings in Orlando's African American community include the Gabriel Jones House on Terry Street, built in 1907, and the Crooms House on Washington Street, built in 1905. The Hill-Tillinghast House on Washington Street, constructed in the early 1920s, has been a meeting place for historical figures such as educator Mary McLeod Bethune and aviator Bessie Coleman.[34]

With the exception of Native Americans, no ethnic group has had a longer association with Central Florida than people of Hispanic descent. Central Florida was mostly an uninhabited wilderness until the mid to late 1800s, when permanent communities began to be established. Small groups of Miccosukee and Seminole Indians lived in the area but did not create lasting settlements here. In fact, when the United States acquired what was to become the state of Florida from Spain in 1821, fewer than eight thousand people lived in the entire region, and most of them were in North and South Florida.[35]

Archaeological discoveries indicate that Paleoindian people resided periodically in Central Florida as long as twelve thousand years ago.[36] These Native Americans had the region to themselves until the early sixteenth century, when Latin culture began to have an impact on the area. The state of Florida owes its very name to the Spanish explorer who "discovered" the area. Spanish colonial administrator Juan Ponce de Leon came to the region in 1513 looking for gold (there is no direct evidence to support the popular myth that he was searching for the fountain of youth) and was so impressed with the diversity of beautiful plant life that he called the area "Florida," which means "the land of flowers." Although the early Spanish explorers claimed the land that is now Central Florida for their country, they did not establish any permanent settlements here.

To protect Spanish trade routes, Pedro Menéndez de Avilés established the first permanent white settlement in North America at St. Augustine, just north of Central Florida. A few days after St. Augustine was established in 1565, Menendez and his colonists marched to what is now Port Royal, South Carolina, to destroy a French settlement there, protecting Spanish claims on Florida.

Spanish control of Florida continued until the mid-eighteenth century. The British gradually began moving into Florida, and when they captured Cuba in 1762, Spain agreed to trade Florida for control of Cuba. The British reigned in Florida for only twenty years, but it was during this time that the first permanent settlement was established in Central Florida. England financed a colony of Italians, Greeks, and Minorcans in 1767 at New Smyrna Beach.[37]

Spain regained control of Florida in 1783, but by 1819 the United States had claim to the territory. Florida was named a state in 1845. Over the next century Hispanic people gradually continued to move to Central Florida, along with settlers of all races and ethnic backgrounds. In the mid to late twentieth century the Latin population of the area steadily began to increase as people from Puerto Rico, Cuba, Mexico, and various South American countries moved to Central Florida to escape oppressive or unstable governments, or to find better economic opportunities. By 1995 the Latin population of Central Florida reached more than a quarter of a million people, with that number expected to double by the turn of the century.[38]

When Rene Plasencia came to Central Florida in 1971, he found a small but close-knit Latin community hungry for a taste of their native culture. Plasencia began a career of promoting Latin dances, galas, and family-oriented festivals that feature Hispanic food, music, and dance. The most successful and well known event presented by Plasencia is the Fiesta Medina, held annually in Orlando's Festival Park. While other local festivals such as Latin Fiesta celebrate Hispanic culture, Fiesta Medina is the only one specifically tied to Orlando history through its affiliation with Medina's Grocery. Plasencia's company, Rene's Productions, is dedicated to preserving Latin culture in Central Florida.

In the early 1960s Rene Plasencia was jailed in Cuba for protesting against Fidel Castro's communist government. Following his release from jail, Plasencia continued his opposition to Castro's regime and was again threatened with imprisonment. Plasencia sought refuge in the Uruguayan Embassy in Havana for ten months, and in the summer of 1963, he and three hundred other Cubans received safe passage to Miami, Florida. Plasencia then spent eight years in Los Angeles before permanently coming to Orlando. In 1971 Plasencia organized the first Latin dance to be held in the area, bringing in bands from Miami and Tampa.

Plasencia remembers beginning his career of preserving Latin culture: "People was crying, just the small amount of the Hispanics that was in Orlando, they was crying to see something like that, and I give to them what they wanted to have. At that time people would go to Tampa or Miami to go to a nightclub or to go to a fiesta. When I came to Orlando, I was able to provide to the small community at that time what they wanted to see, hear, and eat. At that time they were like a small family. We all knowed each others and we all had a good time because the community was real small."[39]

After producing many successful Latin dances and galas, Plasencia turned his attention to presenting family-oriented events. As Central Florida's Latin population continued to swell, so did attendance at Plasencia's events. Today Plasencia presents between seven and ten Latin festivals every year throughout Central Florida. All of his events feature Hispanic food and music and have activities aimed at children. Plasencia feels it is important to attract children to his events so they can be exposed to the culture of their parents and grandparents. Plasencia also operates a nonprofit organization, called the Three Wise Kings, that annually presents a free festival for children and senior citizens and that offers toys and services to children and seniors in need.

The annual Fiesta Medina is Plasencia's most popular and well attended event. In 1987 Plasencia helped his longtime friend Rafael Medina organize a street party to thank the patrons of Medina's market on Bumby Avenue in Orlando. Plasencia explains how Fiesta Medina began: "Medina had always been giving to the customers, the clientella, a small present on Christmas, and once in a while on weekends a party. He was always happy because the Hispanic people make Medina. One day we was talking and there was a decision to have a festival, a big party by Bumby Street, in front of Medina's. We went to all the authorities, and we closed down the street. Surprise for us, there was about five thousand people the first time. It was so successful that Bill Frederick, the Orlando mayor at that time, said that next year it would be even bigger, and we need to change it from the street. Then he gave to us what is today the Festival Park."[40]

The Fiesta Medina was the first event to be held in the Festival Park, a two-block section of grass near downtown Orlando. Plasencia felt that the park should be named after Rafael Medina, since the Fiesta Medina established the area as a festival ground, but the local government did not follow the suggestion. Between forty thousand and fifty thousand people attend the Fiesta Medina every year, free of charge, to hear popular Latin bands from many different countries and to sample Hispanic food prepared by local vendors.

Medina's Grocery on Bumby Avenue in Orlando has been patronized by the local Latin community for many years. The annual Fiesta Medina grew out of a street party that store owner Rafael Medina threw for his customers. Today, tens of thousands of people come to Orlando Festival Park every year to enjoy Latin food, music, and dance at Fiesta Medina.

With the steady increase in the population of Central Florida's Hispanic community, Rene Plasencia's Latin festivals are becoming an essential tool for the preservation of Latin culture in the area. While Plasencia understands the importance of Latin Americans to be integrating into the larger community, he feels they must also continue to respect and treasure the culture of their ancestors. Plasencia hopes that more Anglo Americans will begin to attend his festivals and events, to learn about and experience Latin culture.

Of course many Anglo Americans in Central Florida recognize the value of learning about Latin culture and welcome opportunities to expand their understanding of and appreciation for Hispanic art, music, dance, and food. A growing number of non-Hispanic people attend Fiesta Medina every year, as well as events presented by the Mexican Consulate in Orlando.

In the summer of 1995, the Mexican government established a consulate in Orlando to serve the approximately 350,000 Mexican people living in Central Florida. The consulate regularly displays work by Mexican artists at local museums and galleries. The traditions of Mexico are frequently celebrated through concerts and folkloric performances sponsored by the Mexican Consulate, and Mexico's Independence Day is celebrated in Orlando's Lake Eola Park.

Hispanic roots in "the land of flowers" are deep, and as the Hispanic population of Central Florida continues to grow, the influence of Latin culture is expanding. Cultural events like Fiesta Medina, held in April, and Mexican Independence Day, held in mid-September, give both Hispanics and non-Hispanics an opportunity to celebrate and experience Latin traditions.

In recent decades people of all races and ethnic backgrounds have been moving to and visiting Orlando. The construction of Disney World and its adjacent theme parks led to an explosion of growth in Central Florida in the late twentieth century. The greater Orlando area now includes many towns that were originally separated from the city by wooded areas, farms, and orange groves. While the urban sprawl of Orlando has enveloped many nearby towns, some of these communities retain a sense of individuality. As we continue our look at the cultural heritage of Central Florida, we will visit Winter Park, one of Orlando's nearest neighbors.

❈ Winter Park

The Cultural Heart of Central Florida

Located just a few miles from downtown Orlando, Winter Park is the heart of Central Florida culture. The town's short main street, Park Avenue, is the home of the Charles Hosmer Morse Museum of American Art, several small galleries, and one of the country's major outdoor art festivals, which attracts artists from around the world. Park Avenue ends at the campus of Rollins College, where an annual Bach Festival is presented and an intimate outdoor art festival featuring Florida artists is held. The Annie Russell Theater on the Rollins campus hosts important musical and theatrical performances and high-quality student productions. Travel writer Arthur Frommer has named the Cornell Fine Arts Museum at Rollins "one of America's top ten free attractions" because of the museum's impressive permanent collection, which spans more than five centuries of visual art.[1]

When farmer David Mizell built a log cabin in 1858 on the site of what is now downtown Winter Park, Central Florida was mainly unsettled open space.[2] Florida had been named a state just thirteen years earlier and would secede from the Union in another three years, at the start of the Civil War. Mizell and his family of ten children encountered few white settlers, and the Seminole Indians had been forced out of the area a decade and a half previously by the United States government.[3]

In the early 1880s, Loring A. Chase and Oliver E. Chapman bought much of the land that was to become Winter Park, in

the hope of developing a seasonal-resident community for northerners es-
caping cold weather.[4] Over the next few years a railroad station and several
hotels were built, and Winter Park became a favorite vacation destination
for wealthy people, including President Grover Cleveland and George West-
inghouse. In 1885, Rollins College was built by the Congregational Church,
helping to further Winter Park's growth as a community.[5] The college acquired its present emphasis on the liberal arts under the direction of Ham-
ilton Holt, president of the college from 1925 through 1949.[6]

Winter Park was not incorporated as a town until 1887.[7] That same year
the town of Eatonville, located just a short horse-and-buggy ride away, was
the first town to be incorporated by African Americans.[8] Today the borders
of Winter Park and Eatonville meet, but in the late 1880's they were separated by expanses of woods and citrus groves.

Many wealthy benefactors helped contribute to the growth of Winter
Park throughout the twentieth century. They include businessman Francis P.
Knowles, whose name graces the memorial chapel that is the centerpiece
of Rollins College;[9] entrepreneur Franklin Fairbanks, the namesake of one
of Winter Park's major roads;[10] and industrialist Charles Hosmer Morse,
who donated to the city the two blocks of land on Park Avenue now known
as Central Park.[11] Winter Park continues to attract mostly affluent residents
who have the finances necessary to support the town's many cultural
events, maintain its collections of art, and preserve its mostly Spanish Renaissance–style architecture.

A scenic boat tour, which departs from the dock on Winter Park's Morse
Boulevard, takes passengers on an informative tour of the town's three connecting lakes. Tour guides relate that the "Venetian" canals that connect lakes
Virginia, Osceola, and Maitland were built by Winter Park's founders to
facilitate the transportation of logs and building materials. One of the large
homes on the tour belonged to Czechoslovakian sculptor Albin Polášek and
is now a museum housing many of the artist's works. The sculpture *Man
Carving His Own Destiny* depicts a male figure still partially imbedded in stone,
using tools to free himself from the rock. The piece was probably inspired
by the "unfinished" works of Michelangelo currently lining the entrance of
the Academy in Florence, leading up to the sculpture *David*.[12] Polášek's other
works include male and female nudes, religious pieces, and animals.

Man Carving His Own Destiny, by sculptor Albin Polášek (1879–1965), is on permanent display in front of the artist's Winter Park home, which is open to the public. Other works exhibited on the property include sculptures of male and female nudes, religious works, and animals. Some of Polášek's pieces can be seen by passengers on Winter Park's scenic boat tour.

Winter Park's most significant cultural event is the Winter Park Sidewalk Art Festival, an annual tradition since 1959. Every year several hundred thousand people attend the three-day festival held in the town's two-block Central Park. Approximately three hundred artists from across the United States, and sometimes from other countries, compete in nine different categories for more than fifty thousand dollars of prize money. All aspects of visual art are represented at the festival, including oil and acrylic paintings, watercolors, glasswork, sculpture, photography, ceramics, and hand-crafted jewelry.

To accommodate the crowds of people who attend the festival, held in mid-March, Winter Park blocks off a large portion of the town's main street, Park Avenue, and operates shuttle buses from designated parking areas nearby. In addition to the hundreds of booths of visual art, the Winter Park Sidewalk Art Festival also features musical performances by prominent classical and jazz musicians, and a variety of food vendors are on hand.

The Winter Park Sidewalk Art Festival, a juried event, is not only appreciated by the public that attends, it is also well respected by the participating artists. While many new artists are selected to display their work at each festival, some artists are also invited to come back year after year. Artists who win an award are invited back automatically to the following year's festival.

After winning the first-place award in the metal category at the 1995 festival, jewelry artist Laurie Lyall of Bainbridge, Washington, was invited to participate in the event the following year. She also returned in 1997, after applying and being accepted. Lyall works with eighteen-carat gold and sterling silver to create three-dimensional bracelets and other original jewelry. At the 1997 festival, Lyall said that being accepted into the event is an honor for any artist: "This is one of the top shows in the country, absolutely. It was very exciting for me to win in my category because it was the first year that I had been accepted into the show after applying for fifteen years. Then to win first in my category was astoundingly wonderful. So I was able to come back the next year, in 1996, so this is actually the second year that I've been accepted into the show. It's very rewarding and very wonderful. I would say that the Winter Park Festival is very organized. The people are very appreciative and they come out in droves to see the work and also to buy, which is something that makes us all very happy, of course."[13]

Acrylic artist Dennis Davis is from Gary, Indiana, and has a background in architecture and toy design. At the 1995 Winter Park Sidewalk Art Festival, Davis displayed unusual paintings with realistic houses and other buildings placed in abstract settings. A twenty-year veteran of outdoor art festivals, Davis, like many other artists, praises Winter Park's event: "I've done the Grove for about nineteen straight years; I've done the Cracker Center in Boca Raton, a lot of the big-time Florida shows, as well as shows up north too. Winter Park is definitely one of the best shows in the country. The quality is always good, and it draws a good crowd. Some of the other big-time shows have declined because of bad management, but Winter Park is one of the shows that's maintained its integrity, and still has a good following."[14]

Ted Jaslow of Bogota, New Jersey, creates bright paintings of people in motion—dancing, swimming, or talking at a party. At the 1994 Winter Park festival, Jaslow said that showing his work at that event was important to him as a professional artist: "It's a way of being independent and earning a living at what I love, and not being dependent on the gallery scene. At this show you get to meet the people who are going to own your painting, and live with it. It's like knowing where your children are going, which is kind of cool. If you sell through a gallery, it's all third party and your work just goes off somewhere, and you never see or hear of them again."[15]

While the Winter Park Sidewalk Art Festival occurs only once a year, the collection at the Charles Hosmer Morse Museum of American Art can be enjoyed any time. Artist and interior designer Jeanette Genius McKean founded the Morse Museum of Art in 1942 on the campus of Rollins College, but the facility later relocated to Welbourne Avenue. She named the museum in honor of her grandfather Charles Hosmer Morse, who owned most of the land in Winter Park in the early 1900s.[16] Morse contributed Central Park to the town; he also donated the property for City Hall, the First Congregational Church, the Winter Park Golf Course, and the Woman's Club.

Jeanette Genius McKean was married to Hugh F. McKean, who was a 1930 graduate of Rollins College and an art instructor there beginning in 1932. Hugh McKean served as the president of Rollins from 1952 until 1969.[17] In addition to his career in academia, McKean worked as the director of the Morse Museum from its founding until his death in May 1995. McKean died just two months before the grand opening of the greatly expanded Charles Hosmer Morse Museum of American Art on Park Avenue.

It is no accident that the bulk of the Morse Museum collection consists of the work of Louis Comfort Tiffany. Following his graduation from Rollins, McKean was awarded a fellowship to study with Tiffany at Laurelton Hall, the artist's home and studio in Oyster Bay, Long Island. Tiffany is best remembered for his creative work with stained glass, but he was also a gifted painter. Tiffany's father was Charles Louis Tiffany, founder of the famous New York jewelry store.

In 1992, Hugh McKean remembered Tiffany's philosophy on art: "Mr. Tiffany believed very strongly that the more people you could reach with art, the better off everybody would be. It's difficult to put into words, except I would say that he thought that it was necessary to know art to live a

The Charles Hosmer Morse Museum of American Art, which moved to the current Park Avenue location on July 4, 1995, houses an extensive collection of stained glass works by Louis Comfort Tiffany, including lamps, vases, candlesticks, vessel structures, and windows. Also displayed at the Morse Museum are decorative pieces, furniture, pottery, and paintings.

complete life, or a satisfactory life. He believed that you could put beauty into anything. Wood, crystal, paint, gardens, mosaics, anything, and that you could make it beautiful. He had no quarrel at all with business methods, and he had no quarrel with money. He liked money and he liked to spend it, and he liked to make money. He thought that you'd get them in art galleries, you get them in church, you get them in their houses by hanging a picture on the wall, but you'd [also] get them by doing the whole house, so he said to his associates, 'There's money in this and I'm going to go after it, and I'd like to have you come along and we'll all go after it.' What he meant was that he was going into an interior decorating business, and in a big way he did."[18]

The Charles Hosmer Morse Museum of American Art owns the most comprehensive collection of Tiffany's work to be found anywhere. Tiffany lamps, vases, candlesticks, vessel structures, and other glass works are presented in rotating displays, along with the artist's paintings. On permanent display is the massive emerald-green "Electrolier," a ten-foot-tall electric chandelier Tiffany designed in 1893, as well as many of his most famous stained-glass windows.

After a fire at Laurelton Hall in 1957, Jeanette and Hugh McKean went to Long Island and saved much of Tiffany's work from possible obscurity or destruction. Hugh McKean describes retrieving the art: "My wife, Jeanette, liked it. Her parents had been given Tiffany glass as wedding presents. So we went to Oyster Bay. We looked over all of the place, all of the wreckage. There was just blackened pipes and things standing up against the sky; it was a disaster. It looked like—well, the place was burned up. Curiously, happily, someone, some bright person had taken a lot of the windows out and piled them up in the chapel. The chapel was a little building by itself. So Jeanette said, 'We must take everything here and bring it to Winter Park, Florida.' We were running the Morse Gallery on the Rollins College campus, and I was director and chief, and director of exhibitions. Curiously enough, all these—what he considered his masterpieces—things that had stunned the world with their beauty, all that's left of them is down here in Winter Park, Florida.[19]

While the works of Louis Comfort Tiffany are the focal point of the Charles Hosmer Morse Museum of American Art, collections of American art pottery, nineteenth-century furniture, decorative arts, and paintings by artists such as George Inness, Maxfield Parrish, and Thomas Doughty are also displayed.

Another important figure in the cultural development of Winter Park and Central Florida is John Tiedtke. Originally from Toledo, Ohio, Tiedtke vacationed in Florida with his family in the 1920s. In the 1930s he became very wealthy in Florida's sugar industry, by buying economically depressed land that he later used to turn a profit by growing sugar cane. In 1948 Tiedtke and his wife decided to make Winter Park their permanent home.[20]

Soon after being named treasurer and business manager of Rollins College, Tiedtke saved the institution from financial ruin by securing gifts and loans to cover a $250,000 debt. Tiedtke immediately became active in the local arts and culture scene, helping to establish the Florida Symphony Orchestra and serving on its board of directors until its demise. Although the orchestra folded forty-three years after its first concert, Tiedtke is philosophical about the loss: "There's so many things that have changed since the 1950s. The community is an entirely different community, and what was then something that people liked to listen to, I think that during the last ten, fifteen, twenty years of the orchestra, people had gotten so used to listening to great orchestras on the radio and recordings and things, that the local orchestra no longer sounded so great. In addition to the fact that it was just fairly attended in the Bob Carr Performing Arts Center, not any great return, the big problem was that the cost was tremendous. The orchestra had a budget of four million dollars, and it required two and a half million dollars in gifts."[21]

Following the demise of the Florida Symphony Orchestra, the Orlando Philharmonic Orchestra was formed to play for the Orlando Opera Company and Southern Ballet Theater and to present an occasional classical music concert. While the Orlando Philharmonic does fill a significant portion of the void left by the Florida Symphony Orchestra, a substantial season of orchestral concerts is missed by many Central Floridians. FSO founder John Tiedtke, however, has put his support behind the idea of quality, not quantity, joining the board of directors of the Orlando Celebrity Concerts Association (OCCA), an organization that brings some of the world's best orchestras to the area.

The significant impact that John Tiedtke has had on local arts and culture extends beyond Winter Park to encompass all of Central Florida. Tiedtke's financial and managerial contributions have made orchestral music available to all residents and visitors to the area for more than fifty years. Winter Park has also specifically benefited from Tiedtke's influence through his presentation of one of the most respected Bach festivals in the country.

The Winter Park Bach Festival, held in late February on the campus of Rollins College, brings a series of classical music concerts to the area. While the music of Bach is a mainstay of the concerts, music by other composers, such as Vivaldi and Rossini, is also performed. The more than one hundred voices that make up the Bach Festival Choir practice all year for the event. The choir is accompanied by the Bach Festival Orchestra, and gifted vocal and instrumental soloists augment the program.

The annual Winter Park Bach Festival was established in 1935. Tiedtke explains how he became president in 1950: "The Bach Festival was started by a very dynamic woman, a Mrs. Sprague-Smith, and she did a great job of creating it and getting it going. In 1950, she died suddenly. I was on the board, and nobody else on the board wanted the responsibility of trying to run it and keep it going, so I finally agreed to do it. Then, for two or three years, Hugh McKean, the president of Rollins, and I kept trying to find somebody to run it, and we couldn't. He finally suggested that I just take the title of president because I'd been running it anyway, and up to now we still don't have anybody else to run it, so I'm still running it."[22] The festival concerts are performed for consistently sold out houses in the Knowles Memorial Chapel, with additional concerts being performed in the adjacent Annie Russell Theater.

Also on the campus of Rollins College is the Cornell Fine Arts Museum, which formerly housed Hugh and Jeanette McKean's collection of works by Louis Comfort Tiffany. Currently, the Cornell Fine Arts Museum has a permanent collection of more than six thousand pieces of visual art that reflect important movements from medieval times to the present. The Cornell Museum, in conjunction with the Crealde School of Art, also hosts the Winter Park Autumn Art Festival. Arthur Blumenthal, executive director of the Cornell Fine Arts Museum, helps to select the work that will be displayed in the Winter Park Autumn Art Festival. He explains its distinctive-

The Annie Russell Theater and the adjacent Knowles Memorial Chapel on the Rollins College campus are the home of the Winter Park Bach Festival and many other cultural offerings. Established in 1885, Rollins is one of Florida's oldest colleges. Also on the Rollins campus is the Cornell Fine Arts Museum, which has been called "one of America's top ten free attractions."

ness: "There are quite a few art festivals in the area, the most well known being the Winter Park Sidewalk Art Festival in March. The Winter Park Autumn Art Festival is much smaller, is much more select, and is much harder to get into. It features Florida artists, rather than people from all over, and it tends to be a little bit more artistic; it has more paintings and is higher class in a certain way. I'm prejudiced, of course, since it's right here at Rollins, but I really believe that the Winter Park Autumn Art Festival is the best art festival in the area."[23]

That Winter Park is Central Florida's cultural center is attributable to the wealth and generosity of the town's founders and developers and to the sustaining of cultural endeavors by the affluent residents who followed in their footsteps. In the next chapter we will look at Winter Park's less financially endowed neighbor Eatonville, a community that is rich in cultural heritage.

✸ Eatonville

The Zora Neale Hurston Legacy

The rush-hour traffic is steady on Kennedy Boulevard in Eaton-ville, the main street of the first incorporated African American town in the United States, but the traffic would be much heavier today if Orange County leaders had expanded the two-lane road into a five-lane highway, as they had planned to do in 1987. The County Commission was persuaded not to reconstruct Kennedy Boulevard by the residents of Eatonville, who said the highway would destroy the small 107-year-old municipality made fa-mous by writer Zora Neale Hurston.[1]

The fight to save Eatonville was led by the Association to Preserve the Eatonville Community (P.E.C.), an organization founded and directed by N.Y. Nathiri. She explains the mission of the association: "To give the most accurate characterization of our preservation work in Eatonville, instead of focusing on an individual, one should really focus on the civic pride that re-sides in this community, that resided here as I experienced it as a young child and going into adulthood, and the civic pride that is still here. What I simply did was to express it, and then we collectively found a way to make certain others understood it for what it was. As a community we were unwilling to have a governmental action take our heritage and take away the ability for others to come here and experience and appreciate that heritage. If anything distinguishes our preservation work here in Eatonville, it is that unwillingness to let others dictate our destiny."[2]

Eatonville has earned a place in history by being the oldest town in the United States founded and governed by African Americans,[3] and it was placed on the National Register of Historic Places on February 3, 1998. The early days of Eatonville have been preserved in the writings of Zora Neale Hurston, who lived there as a child. Hurston's most famous novel, *Their Eyes Were Watching God*, is set in Eatonville, as is much of her autobiography, *Dust Tracks on a Road*, and the book *Jonah's Gourd Vine*.[4] Although Hurston died penniless and forgotten in 1960, in recent decades her work as a writer, folklorist, and anthropologist has been experiencing a resurgence in popularity.

Reliable sources indicate that Zora Neale Hurston was born in 1891, although she frequently lied about her age, sometimes shaving off more than ten years.[5] She claimed to have been born in Eatonville, but she stretched the truth a bit there too. Family records indicate that while Hurston was raised in Eatonville, she was actually born in Notasulga, Alabama. Regardless, Hurston considered Eatonville home. The town and its inhabitants fig-

Although the building has undergone significant renovations over the years, the St. Lawrence A.M.E. Church has been in Eatonville since the town was established. Inside the church are murals with religious themes created by André Smith. Smith founded an artists' colony in the town of Maitland, Eatonville's neighbor.

ure prominently in both Hurston's fiction and her work as an anthropologist. Growing up in a town entirely governed by African Americans gave Hurston a strong sense of identity and a belief that she could accomplish her goals.[6]

Although her father cautioned Hurston about being too ambitious, her mother encouraged young Zora to "jump at the sun."[7] While attending Howard University as an English major, Hurston was encouraged to write by professor and African American literary figure Alain Locke. Hurston's first published work was the short story "Drenched in Light," which appeared in a 1924 issue of *Opportunity* magazine. The following year Hurston entered a literary contest sponsored by the Urban League in New York, receiving prizes for both the short story "Spunk" and the one-act play *Color Struck*.[8]

After moving to New York, Hurston received a scholarship at Barnard College, where she majored in anthropology under the renowned Franz Boas.[9] Following her graduation from Barnard in 1928, Hurston collected folklore in Harlem and the southern United States, and also conducted research in the West Indies and Haiti.[10] While living in New York, Hurston became a central figure of the Harlem Renaissance, along with poet Langston Hughes, writer Wallace Thurman, and other African American literati, whom Hurston good-naturedly referred to as the "niggerati."[11]

Hurston's literary output includes many short stories, articles, and dramatic works. In addition to her autobiography, *Dust Tracks on a Road*, Hurston published two collections of folklore, *Mules and Men* and *Tell My Horse*. Hurston's four novels are *Jonah's Gourd Vine*, the story of an unfaithful man with an understanding wife; *Moses: Man of the Mountain*, an examination and retelling of the biblical story of Moses; *Seraph on the Suwanee*, Hurston's only book that features white people as main characters; and the highly acclaimed *Their Eyes Were Watching God*. Published in 1937, *Their Eyes Were Watching God* is generally considered to be Hurston's best work. While telling the story of Janie Crawford's attempts at self-realization, Hurston brings early-twentieth-century Central Florida to life.[12]

Communities that today imperceptibly blend together as the Orlando area are given unique characteristics by Hurston in much of her writing. Retaining the community identity of Eatonville, described in Hurston's work, is a primary goal of the Association to Preserve the Eatonville Community. After successfully convincing the Orange County Commission that expanding Kennedy Boulevard would be a bad idea, N. Y. Nathiri and her staff turned their attention to historic preservation. Under Nathiri's direction, P.E.C. presents the annual Zora Neale Hurston Festival of the Arts and Humanities in late January.

Established in 1990, the festival is a multifaceted event inspired by Hurston's work as a cultural preservationist. Academic discussions and public forums explore the impact of Hurston's writing and examine African American culture. Performing-arts events and workshops led by accomplished black artists are also an important component of the festival. An education day features special programs aimed at students and teachers. The culmination of the event is a two-day street festival with music, dancing, storytelling, crafts, food, and a juried art show.

Talented and internationally known writers, scholars, visual artists, and performing artists participate in the Zora Neale Hurston Festival of the Arts and Humanities every year. Hurston biographer Robert Hemenway, Zora Neale Hurston Society founder Ruth T. Sheffy, jazz pianist Marcus Roberts, actor Ossie Davis, choreographer Jeffery Holder, National Endowment for the Humanities chairman Sheldon Hackney, and poet Maya Angelou are just a few of the distinguished scholars and creative artists who have participated in the multidisciplinary cultural event.

Local scholars and artists also have the opportunity to share their insights and talents at the Hurston Festival. Among the many Central Floridians participating in the event are jazz artists Evelyn and Jesse Stone, painter Arthur Lee Dawson, and bronze sculptor Brian R. Owens. Area organizations not affiliated with the Association to Preserve the Eatonville Community often contribute peripherally to the festival, staging related art exhibitions or performances.

Festival director N. Y. Nathiri is pleased with the positive response that the annual event is generating, and she believes the underlying theme of historic preservation is being realized: "Hopefully from this experience people will gain an appreciation of the importance of preserving your roots. For us it's the Eatonville community, but hopefully people will gain an understanding of the importance of heritage. We see that African Ameri-

This small park area on Eatonville's Kennedy Boulevard is a memorial to Zora Neale Hurston. The plaque mounted on the rock in the center of this picture reads, "Zora Neale Hurston, Eatonville's Daughter, 1890–1960, Anthropologist, Folklorist, Writer, 'She Jumped at the Sun,' The Association to Preserve the Eatonville Community, Inc., January 26, 1990."

can culture has survived, even in unfriendly circumstances at times. We see, as a matter of fact, a strength that comes out of that existence that manifests itself in the black aesthetic. What we are trying to do is to examine in scholarly ways, to inform in lay terms, what that means."[13]

One of the many festival speakers examining the black aesthetic and Zora Neale Hurston's contributions to it is writer Alice Walker, best known for her Pulitzer-prize-winning novel *The Color Purple*. Walker was largely responsible for rekindling an interest in Hurston's work, and in 1973 she had a tombstone placed on Hurston's previously unmarked grave in Fort Pierce, Florida. The inscription reads, "Zora Neale Hurston, A Genius of the South, 1901–1960, Novelist, Folklorist, Anthropologist." During the 1990 festival banquet, Walker said: "I am extremely happy to be here. It's so wonderful to see all of you and feel your love for Zora. And beyond your love for Zora, your willingness to try to understand Zora, which I think is very important. It's especially important for us now, because we have to try harder than ever to think the best of people, rather than the worst. To give people the benefit of the doubt, to not condemn them without knowing what is actually happening. If we don't do that, we're going to lose a lot of our people. We've lost a lot of them already."[14]

Actress Ruby Dee, whose credits include the play *A Raisin in the Sun* and the film *Do the Right Thing*, presented an acting workshop at nearby Rollins College as part of the first Hurston Festival. During a break in the workshop, Dee discussed what makes Hurston's writings noteworthy: "The thing that really intrigues about Zora is that she recognized that our intellectuals, our giant imaginations, our brilliant people weren't necessarily the scholars and the middle class. She knew that found in back woods are extraordinary people, who never heard of Ibsen, who are capable of putting the universe in perspective—genius storytellers who could put the elements of life into imaginative contexts, who might not be able to spell or read and write."[15]

Hurston presented many of those backwoods geniuses in her works, writing out their speech phonetically, preserving their dialects. This authentic rendering of early-twentieth-century African Americans has caused some misguided critics to charge Hurston with perpetuating negative racial stereotypes.[16]

Typical of the interesting oral-history panels presented at the Hurston Festivals is one called "Protectors of the Heritage." A featured speaker at the 1992 festival was Dorothy Porter Wesley, who in 1930 was asked to assemble a collection of resource materials by and about people of African descent for Howard University. Because of the lack of existing printed material focusing on African Americans, Wesley explored the attics and basements of people's homes, collecting newspaper clippings, letters, tax reports, and other materials to make historical information available to scholars. While working on her extensive research project, Wesley met Hurston at a dinner party. Wesley recalls: "She came to Howard in 1924 and '25, and I didn't come until 1928, so I missed her. When she was visiting Washington one day, we were both invited to dinner by a book collector named Henry Slaughter. Something happened in the kitchen, and dinner wasn't ready until eleven. I had all evening to listen to Zora Neale Hurston's tales. She had so many of them I just couldn't believe it. They were so unique and unusual. I thought she was a very interesting character."[17]

Wesley added that the Hurston Festival is an important way to preserve African American culture for young people. The other African American historians on Wesley's panel included Charles L. Blockson, whose cultural collection is at Temple University, and Joan Maynard, executive director of the Society for the Preservation of Weeksville and Bedford-Stuyvesant History. The discussion of African American communities continued during the festival's public forums. Cultural preservationist Eleanor Ramsey, who was responsible for having Allensworth (California's oldest African American community) declared a state park, gave the opening address. The communities discussed in the public forums included Afrikville, Nova Scotia; the Lynwood Park section of Atlanta, Georgia; Carthage, Mississippi; and Eatonville, Florida.

The academic discussions at the Hurston Festivals often focus on Hurston's work and ideas, and their relevance to African American culture. Hurston's impact is also explored in a broader context by examining her Harlem Renaissance contemporaries. Topics at the public forums include Hurston's anticipation of contemporary African American feminist thought, the importance of Hurston's anthropological studies, and advice for teachers on making dialect accessible to students.

One of the numerous performers at the Hurston Festivals is actor, singer, and songwriter Oscar Brown, Jr., who appeared at the 1992 event. Brown has been recognized for his ability to portray accurately the black experience in music and theater. As an actor Brown has appeared in the American Playhouse Theater production of *Zora is My Name: The Zora Neale Hurston Story*, the television series *Brewster Place*, and a variety of stage productions. He has directed, produced, and composed many musicals, including the Broadway production of *Big Time Buck White*, *Joy 66*, *Summer in the City of Chicago*, and *Slave Song*. Brown has written and performed more than 450 songs, including "Brown Baby," "Signifying Monkey," and "The Lone Ranger." As part of a creative team, Brown has collaborated with jazz great Miles Davis and with Brazilian songwriter Luiz Enrique.

In an effort to help get the members of a Chicago gang, the Mighty Blackstone Rangers, off the street, Brown enlisted their participation in a musical revue called *Opportunity, Please Knock*. Brown said that part of the reason he was participating in the Hurston Festival is that Zora Neale Hurston's writings had influenced his work: "I consider myself in Zora Neale Hurston's spirit. I was long before I even heard of her. I've been trying to do some of the same kinds of things she did—to reflect, as accurately as I could through my writing, what I heard, what I saw around me. I felt that was every bit as exotic and interesting and beautiful as any other culture. That was particularly true at the point when I started writing seriously back in the late '50s and '60s, when there was a folk song craze. People were singing stuff from all kinds of cultures. I said, 'Why not the alley back there in Chicago?' My act, so to speak, is based on that sort of thing and bits of folklore which I gathered, to which I have to take my hat off to Zora Neale Hurston, because I never heard of these characters until I read about them in her writings."[18]

The performing arts are prevalent at the Hurston Festivals. Master classes and workshops are held, exploring African American contributions to theater, music, and dance. Public concerts and plays are also presented. A reconstructed version of a play that Hurston wrote in the 1930s based on anthropological studies has been performed at the festival several times. The only extant information about Hurston's play *From Sun to Sun: A Day in the Life of a Railroad Camp* concerns when and where it was originally staged. Program notes from the production indicate the particular railroad camp songs Hurston used and the characters she created from her research. Using this basic information, playwright Thomas R. Wilson and N. Y. Nathiri created a new adaptation of Hurston's work.

The show follows a young man, Youngblood, who longs to explore the world outside of the Central Florida railroad camp where he lives and works. The play is really a vehicle to present some of the folklore and anthropological data that Hurston collected. Following Youngblood through a day, we hear the often humorous songs sung by the workers, the nursery rhymes of playing children, the spirituals sung by women doing their daily chores, and the sermon of an itinerant preacher. We see the Caribbean section of the camp and are exposed to more music and rituals. The play ends at a local "juke joint," where the railroad workers and their women sing the blues and dance.

The reconstructed *From Sun to Sun: A Day in the Life of a Railroad Camp* was first presented in the Annie Russell Theater on the campus of Rollins College during the 1993 Zora Neale Hurston Festival of the Arts and Humanities. Directing the play was Elizabeth Van Dyke, who also toured the country performing the one-woman show *Zora Neale Hurston*, by Lawrence Holder. The presentation of *From Sun to Sun* in the Annie Russell Theater was a homecoming of sorts, since Hurston originally presented the play on the Rollins College campus. Van Dyke explains: "In 1933 the Annie Russell Theater did not allow blacks in the theater, so she could not do *From Sun to Sun* there. She had to do it at the Recreation Hall, where no blacks were allowed to attend. In 1993 here we are, full force, in the Annie Russell Theater. It is a great honor and a great responsibility. It is very fitting because Zora was about claiming your history, claiming your legacy. Here we are in 1993, reliving this, and hopefully passing it on to a new generation."[19] As Hurston must have realized when she originally staged this play, presenting anthropological data in an entertaining and emotionally stimulating way makes the information accessible to a much wider audience.

Important and accomplished creative artists are attracted to the Hurston Festival's mission to preserve African American culture. Elizabeth Van Dyke has returned to the event to direct Hurston's play and, as an actress, has brought Hurston to life in the Lawrence Holder theatrical biography *Zora Neale Hurston*. That play begins in New York on Christmas Eve, 1949. Hurston is alone and broke, waiting for a bus to take her back to Florida. In a series of flashbacks, Van Dyke portrays the highlights of Hurston's career and personal life.

Playwright George C. Wolfe has adapted three of Hurston's short stories into a show called *Spunk*. Wolfe directed the very successful Broadway shows *Angels in America, Jelly's Last Jam,* and *Bring in 'da Noise, Bring in 'da Funk,* and he is producer of the New York Shakespeare Festival. After speaking at a Hurston Festival public forum in 1994, Wolfe said: "She's a great American artist, and we in this country have an incredibly sloppy tradition of honoring artists. I think when you are a black artist in this country, there's an added element of race, but by and large in this entire country there's a fundamental disregard for the quality of what artists bring to and put into their work. In Japan, they think of artists as living treasures. We don't have that phenomenon, but we're trying to cultivate that. Zora Neale Hurston is a great American author, the way Hawthorne, Hemingway, and Fitzgerald are great American authors. She needs to be deified because she contributed to and transformed the landscape of American literature."[20]

Addressing how Hurston's work has helped to make southern black culture a world culture, Wolfe said: "Her work has transformed the world. It is valued and appreciated all over the world. It's a phenomenon of racism in this country that you denigrate something and at the same time export it around the world. That duality needs to end. The more that African American people can claim with arrogance their culture, the less that phenomenon is going to happen."[21]

Glenda Dickerson also participated in the Hurston Festival's academic discussions. Dickerson heads the Drama Department at Spellman College and, like George C. Wolfe, has adapted Hurston's writings for the stage. She remembered her first encounter with Zora Neale Hurston's work: "In 1972 I was living in Washington, D.C., and I went into the People's Drug Store on Fourteenth Street, and I saw a novel that had a black woman on the cover. It cost ninety-five cents, and it was called *Their Eyes Were Watching God*. So I bought it, not thinking anything about it. I read it, and my life was transformed. At the time I had been asked to direct a show at Theater Lobby in Washington, and I asked if instead of doing the show they wanted, if I could do an adaptation of this novel. That's how my production of *Jump at the Sun* came to the stage. Both Alice Walker and Angela Davis, who were in the house when we opened it in San Francisco, said to me that they thought that it was the definitive production of *Their Eyes Were Watching God*. So it transformed my life, the lives of the cast, and the lives of the people who saw it."[22]

Every year, the culmination of the Zora Neale Hurston Festival of the Arts and Humanities is the weekend street festival portion of the event, which brings thousands of people to Eatonville. The crowds examine dozens of displays of African art and clothing, browse through tables of books by and about African Americans, visit booths with craftspeople demonstrating their creations, and sample the offerings of ethnic food vendors. A group of mostly local African American visual artists display their work and compete for prizes. Rows of tables and booths exhibit original jewelry, soapstone boxes, ebony carvings, water carriers, colorful clothing, and craft work. Coconut-shell and animal-bone necklaces, brass items from Ghana, hats and cloth from Nigeria, and various art objects from Africa are also available for purchase. Food vendors offer traditional southern cooking, Caribbean food, and African cuisine. A popular favorite among the culinary choices is Deborah Chester's family recipe for conch and crab fritters served with spiked rice.

At the 1991 festival David E. Wharton exhibited a unique assortment of memorabilia, including a "Wallace for President" license plate, antique Aunt Jemima Breakfast Club pins, and historic images of African Americans in advertising. Wharton explains: "What we've done is present pieces that show nonflattering images of black people. We've got the original Morton Salt girl, Cream of Wheat pieces, and sheet music that has rather derisive pictures on the front. We encourage everybody to look at them, because this is really a true picture of America's past."[23] Another popular display at the street festival features videotapes and pictures of Martin Luther King, Jr., and Malcolm X. Many people also have enjoyed an exhibit of black porcelain dolls. A wide variety of artwork is displayed in the juried art show, including embroidered art, oil paintings, watercolors, and sculpture. The traveling multimedia exhibit "Jump at the Sun" features photographs and documents chronicling the life of Hurston and the history of Eatonville.

Performances on the festival stage include local musicians like Jacqueline Jones and the Bernie Lee Trio, dramatic readings, dance presentations, and storytelling. Festival-goers also take advantage of a guided tour of Eatonville and surrounding points of interest associated with Zora Neale Hurston. Hurston's sorority, Zeta Phi Beta, hosts Children's Corridor activities, including storytelling, face painting, and puppetry. The street festival is enjoyed by a predominately black, yet ethnically diverse crowd.

As the Zora Neale Hurston Festival of the Arts and Humanities progresses into the twenty-first century, it will continue to explore and define the black aesthetic, presenting forums on prominent figures of the Harlem Renaissance and other important African American artists, and active celebrations of culture. In addition to the annual Hurston festivals, the Association to Preserve the Eatonville Community sponsors an annual Summer Performing Arts Workshop for children, an Institute for Teachers that emphasizes interdisciplinary studies, and the Zora Neale Hurston National Museum of Fine Arts, which displays work by black artists from around the world.

The Central Florida that Zora Neale Hurston wrote about no longer exists. The traveler driving down Interstate 4 can pass through Maitland, Eatonville, and Winter Park in just a few minutes, with no significant change of

The Zora Neale Hurston National Museum of Fine Arts is also the headquarters of the Association to Preserve the Eatonville Community, which produces the annual Zora Neale Hurston Festival of the Arts and Humanities. Rotating exhibitions in the museum display works by students, mid-career artists, and established artists of African descent.

scenery. Through the Zora Neale Hurston Festival of the Arts and Humanities, Eatonville is preserving its unique character and sharing it with the world. The "lying porch" of Joe Clark's store has been replaced by a modern grocery, and the Macedonia Missionary Baptist Church, where Hurston's father preached, has been relocated, but Eatonville retains its sense of community.[24] N.Y. Nathiri says: "The one thing that people say is still extant in Eatonville is the community spirit. The buildings mostly are gone, the road is paved over, but the warmness, the spirit, the way of life that Zora Neale Hurston depicted in her writing is still here. It beckons people. In this time when we are all so transient, and the security of relationships is not so easy to come by, we have that in Eatonville. We are fighting drugs and other twenty and twenty-first-century problems that everybody is fighting, but yet and still, that security of relationship, that smallness, that sense of neighborliness, is still here and is what makes this community so appealing."[25]

While urban sprawl envelops much of Central Florida, and a transient population has difficulty feeling a sense of community, Eatonville stands apart as a place where people feel a tie to the past and are planning carefully for the future.

❋ Maitland

The Home of *André Smith* and the *Enzian Theater*

Maitland, like many Florida towns, grew up around the site of a fort constructed during the Seminole Indian Wars. Although the area was reserved for the exclusive use of the Seminoles in the Treaty of Fort Moultrie, signed in 1823, the United States reclaimed the land by building Fort Maitland in 1838. The fort was named in honor of Captain William Seton Maitland, a soldier recognized for gallantry in battle by President Andrew Jackson.[1] A sign marking the site of Fort Maitland was placed on Highway 17–92 in 1935.[2]

Fort Maitland was abandoned in 1842, and settlers began homesteading the area during the following decades. In 1873, pioneer George H. Packwood bought forty acres of land in Maitland, where the town's business and cultural center was established.[3] Developer William H. Waterhouse moved to Maitland from New York in 1884. The Waterhouse home on Lake Lily is listed on the National Register of Historic Places and is now a museum operated by the Maitland Historical Society.[4]

The city of Maitland was incorporated in 1885, two years before its nearest neighbor, Eatonville. The first mayor of Maitland, Tony Taylor, and the town's first marshal, Joe Clark, were instrumental in the creation of America's oldest incorporated African American town. While many people of the era were wary of selling land to African Americans, white Maitland resident Josiah Eaton sold twenty-two acres of land to the settlers of Eatonville, which included Taylor and Clark.[5]

As artist and architect André Smith traveled through Central Florida in the early 1930s, it is possible that he passed through Eatonville on his way to Maitland. Smith may have overheard the residents of Eatonville discussing the success Zora Neale Hurston was experiencing in New York.[6] In any event, Maitland was where Smith would leave his artistic mark.

Today Smith's plan for encouraging the development of American art lives on at the Maitland Art Center in buildings that he designed as an artists' colony. Members of the Central Florida community can explore their artistic talents at the Center's classes; resident artists work in private studios there; the galleries host rotating exhibitions of contemporary American art; and frequent special events such as jazz concerts and dance recitals are presented.

André Smith was born in Hong Kong to American parents. His father was the captain of a naval ship that happened to be in the Pacific when Smith was born. Four years later Smith's father died at sea, and he and his mother moved to Germany. A few years after that, the family relocated to New York, where Smith was raised, and eventually they settled in Connecticut.[7]

Although Smith's first love was art, he earned both a bachelor's degree and a master's degree in architecture from Cornell University at the insistence of his mother, who did not believe that art was a serious way for her son to make a living. Throughout his college career Smith continued to create drawings, engravings, and etchings. Smith's art ranges in style from the realistic to the abstract, which might explain the functional yet fanciful architectural elements incorporated in the Maitland Art Center.

After graduating from college, Smith received a fellowship to study art in Europe. He was the first of eight artists selected by the United States government to go to France with the American Expeditionary Forces in 1918, to record their activities through his drawings and sketches. After World War I, Smith published one hundred of his drawings in a book called *In France with the American Expeditionary Forces*. Smith then received a commission to design the Distinguished Service Cross, which is still awarded today. In 1924 Smith lost a leg as the result of an ignored injury that he had received during officer training seven years earlier.

Smith returned to Stony Creek, Connecticut, after the war, where he designed theater sets for the Parish Players. His experience as a set designer led Smith to write and illustrate *The Scenewright*, published in 1926. Smith enjoyed Connecticut, but in the early 1930s he became tired of the cold, snowy winters. Gerry Shepp, executive director of the Maitland Art Center, explains how Smith came to Central Florida: "He was told about this city called Miami, and how it was becoming the place to live, so he started out, headed for Miami. The story goes that he made it as far as Maitland, and happened to be in this area around sunset, and saw the sun setting over Lake Sybelia, which is right to our west. He decided that it was such a beautiful place, that he never went on to Miami. He began to buy a lot at a time here, and built a house here in 1932."[8]

Smith began spending his winters in Maitland, where he became friends with Broadway actress Annie Russell, a professor of theater arts at nearby Rollins College. Smith designed sets and costumes for theatrical productions at the college. Russell introduced Smith to Mary Curtis Bok, who would later become Mrs. Efram Zimbalist, Sr. Bok later donated the Annie Russell Theater to Rollins in honor of her friend.[9]

Smith and Bok shared a passion for the controversial "modern art" that was developing in the early twentieth century. Bok offered to build Smith a laboratory studio where he could experiment with art, but Smith told her that he was more interested in developing an artists' compound. Smith envisioned a research studio where he could invite prominent American artists to live and work.[10]

In 1937, the compound was built, consisting of studios, living quarters, and a gallery. At the time, Smith operated one of only three art galleries in the state of Florida. For five to seven months every winter, the compound was the residence of well-known artists such as Ralston Crawford, David Burlick, Ernest Roth, Milton Avery, Arnold Blanch, Doris Lee, and Harold McIntosh. Across the street from his compound, Smith built an unusual courtyard, garden, and roofless chapel.

Gerry Shepp says that the new buildings intrigued many Central Florida residents: "When André built this, and built a wall around it, it immediately made people wonder, 'What's going on on the other side? We know those crazy artists are down there!' Of course the moment you put a wall around something it intrigues people. André built the walls so that the artists would have privacy, and so they would not be disturbed. He also built a section across the street, across Packwood Avenue, where there's an open-air chapel and an open-air courtyard. That was for recreation and meditation. The public was allowed to come and visit in there. If the artists wanted to mingle with the public, they could go across the street and meet them over there. The artists were expected to be here to work, to produce, to experiment. That was the whole idea behind the Research Studio."[11]

The first thing that most people notice when visiting the compound that Smith designed is the strong influence of ancient Aztec and Mayan art. The stucco buildings of the Maitland Art Center are heavily decorated with stone carvings and bas-reliefs depicting warriors and gods.[12]

At about the same time that Smith was designing and building his artists' colony, some exciting discoveries were being made in Central and South America. Archeologists were uncovering amazing ruins of Aztec and Mayan civilizations at places like Chichen Itza, Mexico. A seventy-eight-foot-tall pyramid that acts as a huge calendar was uncovered, as was an "observatory" built fifteen hundred years before other similar structures, as well as temples dedicated to various gods.[13]

While the influence of Aztec-Mayan culture is evident in the design of Smith's compound, it is unclear why he selected the ancient Mexican motif. Gerry Shepp says there are two prevailing theories: "We know that André Smith never went to Central America, so he never saw the Aztec-Maya cultures. It's always been a mystery to us because he left no written record as to why he chose to decorate the buildings in this manner. The only thing that we can surmise is that because in the 1930s they were uncovering the ruins in Central America, and having been trained as an architect, he would be aware of these things. Also the Art Deco architecture of this period adopted Maya-Aztec influences and designs in a stylized manner. Being an architect, he would have been aware of that, at least we assume, and that may be the reason that he chose that as the theme for the buildings here, knowing that he never went to see them personally. The other thought that some people have expressed is that the Aztec-Mayans were the first true American cultures, and André was very interested in American culture. He did not feel that artists should have to go to Europe to develop a reputation before they were accepted at home."[14]

The entrance to the Maitland Art Center, formerly the artists' compound built by André Smith in 1937. Resident artists lived and worked in the compound until Smith's death in 1959. In the late 1930s, Smith operated one of three art galleries in Florida.

Smith adopted much of the imagery of ancient Central American civilization for the ornamentation of his compound, but he also mixed it with distinctively Christian imagery, creating an unusual visual effect. On one wall of the compound, the visitor may see a stone carving of an Aztec warrior, and directly opposite that may be a Christ figure, or a bas-relief of an apostle or the Holy Family. This curious blend of Aztec-Mayan influence and Christian imagery can be found throughout the complex maze of courtyards and hidden gardens connecting the twenty-two buildings of Smith's artists' colony. Shepp points out that the juxtaposition of seemingly unrelated images and styles permeated Smith's artwork as well as his architectural designs: "André Smith was ahead of his own time. He experimented with abstracts, he experimented with traditional paintings, he experimented in cement carvings, and he didn't do them in periods, he mixed them, he was doing them all at the same time. His mind must have been fascinating, and must have been going full tilt all the time."[15]

Smith selected a group of five to eight artists to live and work at his compound every year from 1937 until his death in 1959. The buildings were dormant for ten years after that and were in danger of being torn down. In 1969 the property was purchased by the city of Maitland and was maintained as a public trust. In 1971 the compound was leased from the city by the Maitland Art Association and was reopened as the Maitland Art Center.

Today the Maitland Art Center keeps André Smith's dream of promoting contemporary American art alive by offering art classes and workshops, providing work space for two resident artists, and presenting art exhibitions in the gallery space of the compound. In 1982 the Maitland Art Center was placed on both the State and the National Register of Historic Places.[16] Performing-arts programs are often presented on the property, and weddings are held in the open-air chapel. Many artists claim to have seen Smith's ghost wandering the compound and to have been inspired by the benevolent spirit.

When André Smith designed and built what is now the Maitland Art Center, the town's main street was a dirt road that met Winter Park's main street, Park Avenue, which was also a dirt road. Near the point where those

This outdoor chapel and the adjacent courtyard are across the street from the Maitland Art Center. Smith juxtaposed Aztec-Mayan and Christian imagery throughout his artists' compound. Today the chapel and courtyard are used for weddings and public gatherings.

two roads still meet today is the Enzian Theater, an institution dedicated to encouraging and preserving a more contemporary Florida art form: film-making.

The ambience of the Enzian Theater is more like that of a large, comfortable home than of a traditional cinema. The audience sits at small tables and can enjoy either a gourmet dinner and wine or the traditional popcorn and soft drinks. The Enzian screens independent and art films shown nowhere else in Central Florida, as well as historically significant films and foreign films. The theater stimulates filmmaking in the community by showing locally produced work and by hosting the annual Florida Film Festival.

Winter Park philanthropist John Tiedtke built the Enzian Theater in 1985 for his daughter Tina, but his daughter-in-law Siegrid Tiedtke soon took over as manager and director. Under Siegrid Tiedtke's direction the Enzian has become a major cultural resource. In addition to the regularly sched-uled films presented at the Enzian, the theater hosts the annual Brouhaha Festival, which focuses exclusively on films and videos produced by Florida filmmakers. This important event provides an opportunity for both film students and struggling professional filmmakers to show their work.

Perhaps the greatest cultural contribution that the Enzian Theater makes to Maitland and the Central Florida community is the annual Florida Film Festival. For ten days every June, more than one hundred films are pre-sented at the theater and on the Rollins College campus. The festival attracts many film industry leaders and celebrities, such as directors Oliver Stone, Robert Wise, and George Romero and actor and director Dennis Hopper. The festival concludes with an awards ceremony and party hosted by Uni-versal Studios Florida.

For months before the festival begins, Siegrid Tiedtke and her staff screen hundreds of submissions from around the world. As Tiedtke points out, the Florida Film Festival not only gives the Central Florida community a unique opportunity to see stimulating cinema, it also promotes the area as a good location for the production of film: "The Florida Film Festival has a very good reputation outside of Orlando, and that's very important to the filmmaking community here. Filmmakers in the filmmaking communities of L.A. and New York know about the Florida Film Festival and admire it. As well, it's a great chance to showcase the community. All of these filmmakers

The Enzian Theater in Maitland looks more like a large house than a theater. The Enzian shows art films throughout the year and is the home of the Florida Film Festival. The theater also sponsors programs to encourage local film production.

who are coming down here may come back here. If they know more about this town, and if they are here during a celebration that's a sophisticated celebration of film, then they've got a focus, and they've got ten days in this community, when they can really feel like it is a filmmaking community. Our film commissioner takes a number of these people on tours of all the production facilities in town, and they're excited about seeing them. We make every attempt to make these connections, so that people who are making films will come back here to make films."[17]

The establishment of Universal Studios Florida and Disney-MGM Studios in Orlando, as well as the creation of film departments at local colleges, has led hopeful people to label Central Florida as "Hollywood East." The animation department at Disney-MGM has contributed to portions of such successful films as *Aladdin*, *Beauty and the Beast*, and *The Lion King*, and television shows such as *Seaquest*, *Allegra's Window*, and *Legends of the Hidden Temple* are produced at Universal Studios Florida. While filmmaker Oliver Stone (best known as director of films such as *JFK*, *The Doors*, and *Platoon*) thinks that Central Florida is developing a substantial filmmaking community, he believes the nickname "Hollywood East" may be a bit optimistic: "I think that you're going to get some studio production, I think you have a nice suburban environment, a good feel for Americana here, but I think 'Hollywood East' will always be New York. I would say that you'll be lesser, but still I think it'll be a steady flow of films here."[18]

Stone's skepticism aside, film and television production in Central Florida is steadily increasing. The focus of the Florida Film Festival, and of the Enzian Theater in general, however, is not on commercial filmmaking. Siegrid Tiedtke is responsible for the artistic aspect of the Florida Film Festival, and her husband, Philip Tiedtke, secures funding for the event.

Philip explains that the theme for each of the festivals is "Film Is Art": "My father has been putting on a Bach Festival for more than forty years; it appeals to a smaller slice of the community. Almost everyone goes to films, or they watch reruns on cable. For a number of reasons, it seems that the Central Florida community is looking for something they can get behind, like they got behind our local basketball team. Part of my goal is to get all elements of the community behind this, to show that this is a community event, to show that the Central Florida community is behind filmmaking, the production and the enjoyment of films.

"Most people, if they sit in a concert hall or they walk into a building with a lot of things hanging on the walls, they know this is supposed to be art. They don't necessarily think that when they walk into a movie theater. If you step back and think about it, you realize quickly that filmmaking is the most expressive, the most flexible, and the most persuasive art form that has ever been created. When Shakespeare wrote plays, he didn't write them for an elitist, overeducated, one percent of the population to go and chuckle very politely to. They were written for every man; they were enjoyable on many levels. What Shakespeare was trying to do was to tell a story, and express something, and communicate something to the audience. That's exactly what filmmaking does."[19]

To further support the idea of filmmaking as an art form, the Enzian hosts workshops and seminars during the Florida Film Festival and throughout the year to inspire artistic excellence in local filmmakers.

While attending the Enzian Theater's Florida Film Festival, Robert Wise agreed to return to Central Florida to work with film students at Valencia

Community College. Wise is best known as the editor of the classic film *Citizen Kane* and as director of the movie musicals *West Side Story* and *The Sound of Music*. Local film students were given a unique opportunity to create a short film under Wise's direction at Disney-MGM Studios. Wise explains: "The film is not to be shown at festivals or on television. It's really a class exercise, and I made a big point with them. I wanted to be sure it would only be used for educational purposes. It will be shown in university and college classes, but not for any real public exposure; that's not the purpose of it. I want to make it as good as I can, as inexpensively as I can, and utilize the talents of the students. I have two or three professionals on the crew, someone from sound, the makeup lady, but all the rest are students learning what it's like to be behind the camera, and to run sound, and to be a grip, an electrician, a prop man, a special effects man, and all the things we do in film."[20]

Both the Maitland Art Center and the Enzian Theater encourage local artists to experiment and push the boundaries of well-established art forms, and both give the community at large an opportunity to view the results of that work. The efforts of these institutions, and a history dating back to the mid-1800s, make the city of Maitland a substantial contributor to the cultural heritage of Central Florida.

❀ Christmas

Remembering the Seminole Indian Wars and Florida's Pioneer Days

Before the English financed Central Florida's first permanent settlement at New Smyrna Beach in 1767, the Seminole and Miccosukee Indians enjoyed a life of peaceful freedom in the area. For fifty years after white people began moving into Florida, no serious conflicts occurred between the native inhabitants and the settlers. Then, in 1817, the United States invaded Spanish-controlled Florida, and the first of three Seminole Indian Wars began.[1]

While the desire to expand the territory controlled by the United States was a motivating factor for the invasion of Florida, the primary reason a conflict with the Seminoles arose was that the Native Americans were protecting runaway slaves who had escaped from their captors in Georgia.[2] When the white slave owners from Georgia came to Florida in search of their lost "property," the Seminole Indians risked their own lives to protect the African Americans who lived among them as workers, favored dependents, and advisers.[3]

The defensive forces of the Seminoles proved to be no match for General Andrew Jackson's well-organized and heavily armed soldiers, and the Native Americans were defeated by 1818. Florida was named a territory of the United States four years later. Although the Seminole Indians had been raising crops, organizing citrus groves, and domesticating cattle in Florida for many years, the United States government decided to push the Seminoles south and enclose them in a reservation.[4]

The 1823 Treaty of Moultrie Creek allowed the Seminoles to live on a restricted area of land. In fewer than ten years, the United States government failed to honor the agreement, deciding to settle the land that they had previously designated for the Seminoles. In 1832 the Treaty of Paynes Landing was signed, which called for the native Floridians to be removed from the state altogether and relocated to the Arkansas Territory west of the Mississippi River.[5]

Many Seminoles thought that the new treaty was unfair and did not believe that the people who had defaulted on the Treaty of Moultrie Creek should be trusted. Seminole leader Osceola refused to sign the treaty and was consequently arrested and imprisoned. Having learned the art of deception from his captors, Osceola pretended he would sign the treaty. After being released, Osceola instead organized a successful campaign of guerrilla warfare against the white invaders.[6]

In 1835, 111 soldiers marched from Fort Brooke, heading for Fort King. Seeing the caravan as another act of aggression, the Seminoles ambushed the soldiers, killing and scalping all but three.[7] The battle, called Dade's Massacre, began the Second Seminole Indian War.[8] During the seven-year war the United States government established a series of forts throughout the state, situated about a day's journey apart, to keep supplies flowing to the soldiers.

In 1837, Fort Christmas was built in east Orange County. In 1977 the Orange County Parks Department constructed a replica of Fort Christmas about one mile south of its original location. The fort is used as a museum honoring the memory of the Seminole Indians who were defending their freedom, the soldiers who fought for American expansion, the runaway slaves who sought refuge in Florida, and the early pioneers who set up communities in the area. Museum guide Vicky Prewett explains how Fort Christmas got its name: "There were two thousand soldiers that were marching and they had seventy wagons that were following them. They were coming from Fort Mellon, which was over in Sanford. When they arrived at Powelltown, a large Indian village that was abandoned, of course, at the time, they built their fort on the opposite side of the creek. They arrived there on December 25, 1837, and that was Christmas Day, so they decided that they would name their fort Fort Christmas."[9]

Fort Christmas consists of a sturdy wooden fence, forming a square with sides eighty feet long, with two high blockhouses on opposing corners. The army officers lived in the blockhouses, while the nearly two thousand soldiers posted at the fort camped outside. In emergencies the soldiers could retreat to relative safety within the fences of the fort. Inside the walls of the fort is a storehouse where supplies were kept and, as Vicky Prewett explains, a powder magazine to store weapons and ammunition: "The powder magazine is where the soldiers stored their gunpowder and any extra muskets that they had. The powder magazine is underground, it's got like a cellar in it, and the reason for that was of course to protect the gunpowder. Their muskets were flintlock muskets, and of course one little spark from the flint of the muskets would ignite the gunpowder and make the musket balls shoot out. Gunpowder is highly explosive, and they needed to protect it

The main blockhouse of Fort Christmas, a replica of the military outpost built in 1837 during the Second Seminole Indian War. The replica of Fort Christmas, built in 1977 by the Orange County Parks Department, is located about one mile south of the fort's original location. On display in the blockhouse are military and Native American artifacts from the time of the Seminole Indian War.

from any sparks. Of course, being underground like that, if it did explode, they were hoping fewer people would be injured because the direction of the explosion would be upward instead of outward."[10]

The storehouse of Fort Christmas currently houses an audiovisual presentation on the Seminole wars, and the blockhouses are used as exhibition space. On the first floor of the first blockhouse are displays of maps, weapons, treaties, soldier uniforms, and other military artifacts from the Seminole-War period. The second floor of the first blockhouse is dedicated to the Seminole Indians, with clothing, crafts, and weapons on display. A recording of a Seminole Indian medicine man allows visitors to hear a healing chant and stories passed down from previous generations.

A few months after the original Fort Christmas was built, a truce in the Second Seminole Indian War was called, and Chief Osceola was invited to attend a peace conference. The truce was just a ruse to lure Osceola into a hostile camp, where he could be captured. Osceola was imprisoned in St.

The powder magazine inside the walls of Fort Christmas. Ammunition and gunpowder were stored in the cellar of this building to minimize damage to the fort in case of an accidental explosion. Only army officers lived inside the walls of the fort. About two thousand soldiers camped outside.

Augustine and was later moved to Fort Moultrie, South Carolina, where he died in captivity in January 1838.[11] Vicky Prewett explains that, although the Second Seminole Indian War would last until 1842, Fort Christmas quickly became obsolete: "Mainly it was a supply depot. What the army tried to do was set up a chain of forts to carry supplies to the soldiers that were fighting south of here, so they tried to situate the forts one day's travel apart. Once the roads and the bridges were constructed, ideally it would take one day to go from one fort to another, so that the supplies never had to be out in the open overnight. That's what they were trying to do when they established the whole chain of forts, but it was just a short period of time in history. We're talking probably about three months that the fort was actually used by the army. They discovered a route by water, and it was much easier to carry supplies by water than to try to carry them through the marshy land of Florida."[12]

The second blockhouse of the Fort Christmas Museum houses displays

A view of the main blockhouse of Fort Christmas from inside the outpost walls. Today, Seminole Indian War memorabilia and Native American artifacts are displayed in this building. The Fort Christmas Park and Museum frequently presents demonstrations of pioneer skills such as syrup-making and quilt-making.

of items used by early settlers of east Orange County, following the Second Seminole Indian War. Exhibited items include farm equipment, tools, household furnishings, and pictures of the first settlers and their descendants. Surrounding the Fort Christmas Museum is a group of reconstructed pioneer houses from the late 1800s through the early 1900s, and equipment from an early sugar mill. Vicky Prewett says that the government offered incentives to the early settlers of Central Florida: "At the end of the Second Seminole Indian War, the Congress passed the Armed Occupation and Settlement Act of 1842. This act gave permits for free land, 160 acres, to any family that would come, stay for five years, build a house, clear and cultivate five acres of the land, and be able and willing to bear arms to protect themselves and their neighbors. Most of the homesteads were ten miles apart, and there were like 1,284 permits issued, and within nine months about a thousand families had picked up these permits."[13]

War Department figures indicate that 3,824 Seminole Indians were shipped west in 1842, and about 300 more fled south to the Everglades. The absence of Native Americans allowed white settlers to feel more confident about moving to Central Florida. The Third Seminole Indian War was fought well south of Central Florida, from 1855 to 1858. Battles arose between the native Floridians and white surveyors. Today more than fourteen hundred Seminoles live on three reservations in South Florida.

Gradually families began to settle permanently in the area now known as Christmas. In 1867 a little girl named Emily Tucker was the first person to be buried in the Christmas cemetery. In 1892 the Christmas post office was established, and that is when Fort was dropped from the name of the community. The town received electricity in 1947, and as late as the 1960s residents shared three pay telephones. For more than one hundred years, the population of Christmas never exceeded 250 people. Today it remains a mainly rural, agriculturally based community.[14]

The Fort Christmas Museum and Park is a valuable educational resource. The fort itself, the pioneer houses in the park, and the exhibitions on display all give the visitor insight about what life was like for the early settlers and original inhabitants of Central Florida. The park frequently sponsors demonstrations of syrup-making, quilt-making, and other activities of local pioneers. Trudy Trask, the historic site supervisor at the Fort Christmas

Museum and Park, says her goal is to maintain a living history park: "Our park now annually has an attendance of a little over 160,000, and a little over 20,000 of those are kids who we do programs for. We serve children from Brevard County, Osceola County, Seminole, Volusia, Orange, and Lake Counties. We have a program for grade-school kids, called our Pioneer Experience Program, and the kids come and camp overnight, and they make pioneer stew, and they do all kinds of pioneer arts and crafts, and hands-on programs. Children seem to forget that videos and computer games and televisions haven't always been here. We're trying to preserve the pioneer way of life, and show them what it was like."[15]

While the Fort Christmas Museum is the primary focus of the park, the Orange County Parks Department has also constructed a covered picnic area, a tennis court, a basketball court, and a baseball field on the ten acres of land.

As with most Central Florida towns, development is gradually encroaching on Christmas. The northern expansion of major highways and expressways threatens to swallow Christmas into the undefined Orlando area, and overflow from the coastal communities of Cocoa Beach and Cape Canaveral is pushing into Christmas from the east. The Christmas post office has been enlarged several times, not only to handle the mail of the town's residents, but to deal with the tens of thousands of Christmas cards brought there every year for the unique postmark and the bags of mail sent to Santa Claus at his Florida address.

Even after the town of Christmas is absorbed into the urban sprawl of Orlando, the Fort Christmas Museum and Park will preserve the early lifestyles of Central Florida residents for future generations. The park honors not only the area's early pioneers, but the Seminole Indians who originally lived here, the soldiers who paved the way for the development of Florida, and the runaway slaves who sought refuge here.

❋ Longwood

A Microcosm of Central Florida History

The city of Longwood has one of the most well preserved historic districts in what is now Seminole County. From 1825 until 1845, most of the Central Florida area was called Mosquito County. A large portion of Mosquito County was renamed Orange County in 1845. By the time Seminole County was carved out of Orange County in 1913, Longwood had been in existence for about forty years.[1] Today the residents of Longwood celebrate the history of their city by preserving historic buildings and by hosting two annual arts and crafts festivals in the historic district.

Early settlers began coming to the Longwood area in the 1870s. Most of these pioneers came to Central Florida on the St. Johns River, arriving in nearby Sanford. The Hartley and Searcy families were some of the first people to call Longwood home. In 1873 a young man named Edward Henck came to the Longwood area and gave the town its name. Henck had helped to design the layout for the Boston suburb of Longwood, and he thought that the name would be appropriate for his new home.[2]

Henck established the first mail route through Longwood in 1876, and he served as the town's first postmaster until 1885.[3] By 1880 Henck had started the South Florida Railroad, and he obtained the charter for the first railroad to be constructed in Central Florida. Under Henck's direction a railroad was built to link Sanford to Orlando.[4] Henck extended his railroad to Kissimmee, which allowed connections to Tampa on the Plant Railroad System. With a railroad system in North Florida leading to the St. Johns River, efficient boat travel down the St. Johns to Sanford, and a railroad leaving from Sanford, Central Florida was opened up to tourism by the late 1880s.[5]

As if establishing a post office and a railroad system were not enough for Henck to do to encourage the growth of Longwood, he also homesteaded the area that is now the historic district and subdivided it for families and businesses to purchase lots. Henck incorporated Longwood as a town in 1883 and served as the first mayor. Throughout the 1880s and early 1890s Longwood had active timber-and citrus-exporting industries that benefited from the railroad Henck built.[6]

Another person who was instrumental to the early growth of Longwood was Peter Demens. Born to a noble family in Russia, Demens was educated in St. Petersburg. Following a brief stint in the Russian army, Demens managed several large family estates. For unknown reasons Demens was forced to flee Russia in 1881, and he came to Longwood.[7]

Although he lived in Longwood for only eight years, Demens was one of the town's most important early citizens. Demens bought an eighty-acre orange grove and one-third interest in a sawmill.[8] Within two years Demens bought out his partners in the sawmill and acquired a contract to build the station houses for the South Florida Railroad. Demens was also hired to construct buildings at Rollins College in Winter Park, which were deemed to be "quite deficient" upon their completion.[9]

While living in Longwood, Demens also received a contract to make the railroad ties for the Orange Belt Railway. The track would run from Lake Monroe to the south side of Lake Apopka and continue to the Tampa Bay area. After many financial setbacks the track was completed and Demens was given the railroad charter instead of payment. The community at the end of the Orange Belt Railway was named St. Petersburg in honor of Demens's hometown in Russia.[10] Building the railroad left Demens in debt, and he sold it in 1889. Demens left Longwood for North Carolina and later moved to California, where he died in 1919.[11]

While Henck and Demens conceptualized and financed most of the construction in the young Longwood community, it was master carpenter Josiah Clouser who actually hammered the nails that hold together most of the buildings still standing in the city's historic district.[12] Clouser brought his wife and two children to Longwood from Pennsylvania in 1881.

John Bistline, a fourth-generation Longwood resident, is the great-grandson of Josiah Clouser's daughter. As Bistline explains, Longwood's early boom-town period was short lived: "The first exciting period in Longwood was in the 1880s up to 1894–95, when the freeze came. At that time Longwood had a thousand people. It was one of the largest, if not the largest place in Orange, later Seminole County. It was largely due to the sawmill. Being a center of population, there were a lot of shops—millinery stores, that type of thing, hardware stores—here in Longwood. Of course the tourists came in the winter. Then after the freeze, which happened about the same time that the lumber ran out around here, the sawmill reduced its size greatly. A number of the people who lived here, that depended on oranges, picked up and left after that. They just no longer continued to be interested in this area and moved elsewhere, so the population shrunk to about three hundred."[13]

The heart of Longwood's historic district is centrally located in a two-block area on Warren Avenue and Church Avenue near the intersection of County Roads 427 and 434. A walking tour of these streets allows the visitor to see a group of well-preserved buildings that were among the first to be constructed in the city.

The Clouser Cottage, located at 219 West Church Avenue, was built in 1881. When Clouser first came to Longwood to work for Henck, he was provided with a home. However, Mrs. Clouser refused to live in the home because it was infested with fleas. Clouser quickly constructed the cottage as a temporary residence using scrap lumber. The building is made of vertical boards and batten siding nailed directly to the interior paneling without structural stud framing. In 1991 the Florida Trust for Historic Preservation awarded the cottage owners a citation, "In Recognition of Meritorious Achievement for Rehabilitation of a Historic Residential Structure." The Clouser Cottage is currently used as a gift shop.

The Clouser House, located at 221 West Warren Avenue, is directly behind the Clouser Cottage. It took four years for Clouser to build the house because he was working on other construction projects at the same time. The wood-frame vernacular-style house was the Clouser family home for many years and more recently has been used as an antique store and a birthing center. Clouser incorporated some unique decorative features into his house, including a Chinese-Chippendale-style handrail and unusual spindle work on the porch.

The Christ Episcopal Church at 151 West Church Avenue is the oldest church in continuous use in Seminole County.[14] Constructed in 1881, the church was dedicated at Easter services in 1882. The board-and-batten siding, square bell tower, and symmetrical plan are typical of early pioneer churches. Two easily identifiable wings were added to the church in 1965. In 1988 the church was moved slightly to make room for additional buildings on the property.

The Inside-Outside House at 141 West Church Avenue is thought to be one of the oldest prefabricated homes in the United States. Built in Boston in 1870, the house was brought to Central Florida by boat.[15] An ox cart was used to bring the house to Altamonte Springs, a community adjacent to Longwood. The builder of the home, Captain W. Pierce, allowed his house to be used as a way station for soldiers in the Third Seminole Indian War until 1878. After the war, Pierce became a cabinetmaker and used the first floor of his home as a shop.

Pierce's home is known as the Inside-Outside House because the structural wall studs are clearly visible on the outside of the building, but are finished on the inside. It is interesting to note a small balcony on the exterior of the house where a staircase formerly led to the second floor. Pierce removed the outside stairs after building a steep spiral staircase inside.

The home was moved to its current location in 1973 by the Central Florida Society for Historic Preservation.[16] In the early 1970s property values in Altamonte Springs were rising dramatically, and the Inside-Outside House was threatened with demolition. If it had not been moved, it would have been torn down to make room for doctors' offices.

Popular legend in Longwood maintains that the Inside-Outside House is haunted by Captain Pierce's cat, Brutus. When Brutus died, Pierce made the cat a casket and buried him in the yard. Ever since the home has been relocated to Longwood, stories about the antics of Brutus's ghost abound. While in Pierce's home, people have reported feeling an invisible cat brush against their legs and seeing a rocking chair move as if a cat had just jumped off.

The Civic League Women's Club, constructed in 1870, is thought to be the

The Inside-Outside House, brought to Longwood in 1872, is thought to be one of the oldest prefabricated homes in America. The fact that structural wall studs are clearly visible on the outside of the building, but are finished on the inside, earned the house its name. Popular legend maintains that the Inside-Outside House is haunted by the original owner's cat, Brutus.

oldest building in Longwood.[17] The multipurpose meeting hall was origi-nally located about a block away from its current home at 150 West Church Avenue. Before being moved to its present location in 1914, the building had been moved to West Longwood. Over the years the Civic League Women's Club building has been used as a chapel, a classroom, a dance hall, a theater, and a library.

The Civic League Women's Club was founded in 1916. The organization's first project was to have streetlights installed in Longwood. After raising the money to purchase the lights, the club paid a boy named Morris Clouser (a descendant of Josiah Clouser) two dollars a week to fill the lamps with kerosene and keep them lit until midnight each night.

The Longwood Hotel is located on County Road 427, between Warren Avenue and Church Avenue. Built in 1886–87 by Josiah Clouser for Edward Henck, the building opened in 1888 as the Waltham Hotel. Following the Big Freeze of 1894–95 the hotel closed until 1910. The hotel was briefly known as the St. George in 1922, but the following year was renamed the Orange and Black. During the 1920s the hotel was a popular gambling house, and in 1929 the National Governors' Conference was held there.[18]

The Longwood Hotel closed again during the Depression and has since been used as a school, a restaurant, and a film location. Since 1983 the hotel has been an office building owned by the Centennial Corporation. Listed on the National Register of Historic Places, the wood-frame vernacular-style building retains Italianate details such as pedimented window heads and eave brackets supporting the roof overhang.[19]

The Bradlee-McIntyre House is the most ornate building in Longwood's historic district and the only remaining winter cottage of its size built in the 1880s. Originally built in Altamonte Springs in 1885, the house was relocated to Longwood in 1973 by the Central Florida Society for Historic Preservation to protect it from demolition.[20] Boston architect Nathaniel Bradlee designed the home as a winter residence for his family. The house was occupied by the McIntyre family from the early 1900s until 1946.

An elaborate example of Queen-Anne-style architecture, the Bradlee-McIntyre House is listed on the National Register of Historic Places.[21] Josiah Clouser helped to build the highly ornamented home. The architectural details of the house include decorated shingles, asymmetrical towers, steeply pitched roofs, and bull's eye carving around the interior doors.

The evolution of Longwood mirrors that of many Central Florida towns, with settlement in the 1880s and continued growth until the Big Freeze of

The Longwood Hotel, built in 1886, now houses offices. In the 1920s the hotel was a popular gambling house. In more recent years the hotel has been used as a school, a restaurant, and a film location.

The Bradlee-McIntyre House, built in 1885, was originally located in Altamonte Springs but was moved to Longwood in 1973. The Central Florida Society for Historic Preservation gives tours of the home. An elaborate example of Queen-Anne-style architecture, the Bradlee-McIntyre House is listed on the National Register of Historic Places.

1894–95. Also typical of many Central Florida communities is the burst of growth experienced by Longwood in the 1920s.

John Bistline explains how the Florida real-estate boom of the 1920s affected Longwood: "During the '20s boom the place picked up like mad. The roads were paved all around. We had a road paved to Oviedo, we had a road paved out to Markham. The main road had been paved, but it was extended. It came through from Sanford, into Altamonte, and on down to Orlando. Warren Street was paved out as far as Sanlando Springs. Subdivisions were laid out all around. We had the Sanford-Orlando Kennel Club come in. The Rolling Hills Golf Course was built out here on the road to Sanlando. The horse track, which is now another dog track, was also built. We had a mile track, and we had betting for a year or two. It was going to be turned into another Miami. The place was laid out all over with subdivisions, but just about that time the bubble broke and people didn't keep coming. Subdivisions stayed, but there were no homes built in them."[22]

Evidence of the optimism prevalent in 1920s Central Florida can be seen in the Henck-Tinker Building, located across from the Longwood Hotel on County Road 427. Financed by Edward Henck and professional baseball player Joe Tinker in 1925, the structure is a typical brick commercial-style building of the period.

The north end of the Henck-Tinker Building was occupied by the city's first bank until 1932. Although the Longwood State Bank has been out of business since the Depression, the vault is still inside the building. Mac-Reynold's Drug Store, Jackson's Grocery, and a barber shop were the building's other occupants for many years. The corner entrance of the bank retains a raised parapet wall and brick detailing, but the south portion of the building has been covered in stucco.

Again reflecting the typical growth patterns of many Central Florida towns, Longwood began a steady period of growth in the 1960s that continues today. The establishment of space-program-related industries and the presence of popular theme parks have attracted hundreds of thousands of people to the area, transforming Longwood and other cities into bedroom communities. The current population of Longwood alone is around 13,500.

The primary objective of this book is to examine historic preservation efforts and cultural celebrations that exploit Central Florida's past in a positive way, contributing to a sense of community. The residents of Longwood recognize the importance of retaining their city's character through the physical preservation of buildings. Longwood residents also host two an-

The Henck-Tinker Building, a typical brick commercial-style building of the 1920s, is located across the street from the Longwood Hotel. The city's first bank was located in the Henck-Tinker Building until the Depression of 1932. The corner entrance of the former bank retains a raised parapet and brick detailing, but the south portion of the building has been covered in stucco.

nual arts and crafts festivals that bring the community together while raising money for historic preservation.

Since the mid-1970s the Central Florida Society for Historic Preservation has sponsored the Longwood Arts and Crafts Festival on the weekend before Thanksgiving. Held on Warren Avenue and Church Avenue in the city's historic district, the event is the primary fundraiser for the society. The funds raised by the festival go toward the maintenance and continued furnishing of the Bradlee-McIntyre House and other projects.

More inclusive than the Winter Park Sidewalk Art Festival, the Longwood Arts and Crafts Festival features hundreds of booths with handmade jewelry, woodwork, homemade clothing, ceramics, and quilts. Food vendors also add to the festival atmosphere.

Inspired by the success of the Longwood Arts and Crafts Festival, the Historic Preservation Board of the City of Longwood instituted the annual Founder's Day Spring Arts and Crafts Festival in March 1996. Very similar to the fall festival, the Founder's Day event is also held in Longwood's historic district. Nelda Pryor, chair of the Historic Preservation Board, explains the objective of the Founder's Day Festival: "This festival is held primarily to raise funds to go directly back into the historic district. The first one of our projects is to put brick into the streets of Longwood in the historic district. We're raising money to offset the cost of the brick as opposed to the blacktop surfacing. Once that's done, we'll move forward and put in some nice lighting that matches the era. Then we'll continue with our bench project and our ongoing engraved-brick project. We sell engraved brick for fifteen dollars apiece. You have three lines of engraving. They will be inlaid in the brick streets. All of the money raised by the Founder's Day Festival goes right back into the historic district."[23]

Much of Longwood looks like any average American suburb. Convenience stores, schools, banks, and a hospital are surrounded by hundreds of contemporary homes. Many Longwood residents commute to work in larger communities nearby. In a time of continued growth and expansion, the Longwood historic district provides residents with a sense of community pride, and the cultural events held there bring people together to celebrate their heritage.

✸ Sanford

An Architectural Archive

Within the three-block area that makes up Sanford's downtown historic district, there are more than twenty buildings that are listed in the National Register of Historic Places. Most of the buildings were constructed in the late 1800s, and the newest one was built in 1923. All of the buildings in Sanford's downtown historic district are remarkably well preserved, and together they create an ambience unique in Central Florida.

Directly adjacent to Sanford's downtown historic district is the residential historic district, which contains many houses that are listed in the National Register of Historic Homes. Most of the homes in this neighborhood were built in the early twentieth century. While the more than four hundred structures in Sanford's residential historic district are gradually being renovated, homes in various states of disrepair sit next to others that have been completely restored to their original beauty. The Sanford Historic Trust is aggressively working to help homeowners refurbish their homes by raising money for renovations and repairs.

Sanford has a long and turbulent history dating from the 1830s[1] and has endured several prolonged periods of economic hardship that have left the town's historic districts virtually untouched by development. Today historic preservationists in Sanford have an opportunity to protect their town's unique and charming character.

Like many Florida towns, Sanford was built around the site of a military camp established in the 1830s during the Seminole Indian Wars. A military fort was constructed at Camp Monroe in 1837 and was named Fort Mellon after Captain Charles Mellon, a soldier who was killed in battle defending the camp. Many early settlers in Central Florida built homes near the fort, and they called their community Mellonville.[2]

As the site of commercial steamboat traffic in the 1840s, Mellonville served as the major distribution point for building materials and other goods needed by settlers throughout Central Florida. Alicia Clark, curator of the Sanford Museum, explains that when entrepreneur Henry Sanford came to the area in 1870, he believed that it could serve as the major port for all of southern Florida: "When Henry Sanford came here in 1870, he was looking for an investment during the Reconstruction period, and he had been advised that Florida was a good investment. He was from Connecticut, and he was a diplomat who had lived overseas most of his life, and he was looking for a good way to invest his money. He came here, he landed at Mellonville, found out there was a large former Spanish land grant to the west of Mellonville, which he purchased for eighteen thousand dollars. It was over twelve thousand acres, and he founded the town of Sanford, which was a planned city drawn out on paper."[3]

As a port city, and later a railroad terminal, Sanford prospered in the late nineteenth century. As a transportation hub for several decades, Sanford was actually a more prominent and prosperous town than its neighbors Orlando and Winter Park.[4] Alicia Clark explains that Sanford's tenure as the focal point of Central Florida was short-lived: "We had a thousand citizens very early on, which for that time period was a lot. We became very quickly the largest inland city in Florida, and also very quickly we were the fourth largest city in Florida. The city grew because of the St. Johns River. We're located on Lake Monroe, which is a wide spot in the St. Johns. It was a two-day trip to Jacksonville, and from Jacksonville you could connect to anywhere. Henry Sanford came here from Belgium. He was living in Belgium, and he could come right to Jacksonville and hook up with the riverboats. The riverboats are what built the city. In 1880 he brought the South Florida Railroad in here, and that made us a transportation hub. He named us 'The Gate City of South Florida,' and we were a gateway city. It's hard to visualize now, but we were a larger, more important place than Orlando, because we had the port. Things changed when the automobile was invented. Henry Sanford had no way of knowing that was going to happen. The riverboat ceased to be quite as important."[5]

Under Henry Sanford's leadership the city of Sanford flourished. In addition to bringing riverboat wharves, a train station, and a hotel to his town, Mr. Sanford developed a citrus grove and experimental garden called Belair.[6] Before the turn of the century, the citrus industry became the most significant economic force in Sanford. In 1880 Mr. Sanford formed the Florida Land Colonization Company in London to encourage European investment in Central Florida.

Following an initial period of prosperity, Sanford faced a series of economic hardships. Henry Sanford lost his fight to have the Orange County seat moved from Orlando to Sanford, but when Seminole County was created in 1913, Sanford was named its county seat.[7] In September 1887 a bakery in downtown Sanford caught fire and destroyed much of the town. Brick buildings were constructed the same year to replace the burnt wooden structures, and many of them still stand today.[8]

The Big Freeze of 1894–95 destroyed the citrus industry in Sanford, but many farmers turned to celery as their primary crop. Early in the twentieth century Sanford exported so much celery ($8 million worth a year) that it was dubbed "Celery City."[9] The Great Depression impacted Florida several years earlier than the rest of the country, and Sanford was nearly crippled.[10]

The economy of Sanford was revitalized in 1942 when the Navy built an air station in Sanford, but the town suffered when the station moved to Orlando in 1968.[11] Following the departure of the Navy, Sanford entered an economic slump that is now slowly waning.

To the delight of cultural preservationists, the historic sections of the city of Sanford escaped the widespread development that caused the destruction of many older Central Florida buildings. The lack of interest in bringing new businesses and corporations to Sanford has allowed the downtown area and its adjacent residential neighborhoods to remain undisturbed. Today, the widespread preservation efforts underway in Sanford will usher in a new era of prosperity because the town will be able to enjoy the benefits of the growing interest in cultural tourism and will attract new residents.

While historic preservation efforts in Sanford accelerated in the 1990s,

Alicia Clark says an interest in protecting the city's past goes back to the mid-1970s, when local residents were inspired by the bicentennial of the United States: "A lot of communities of our size were trying to find something to do to help revive interest in their local history. What they did downtown was to put the commercial district on the National Register. They hired some researchers to go and research the oldest buildings downtown, and they were submitted to Washington, and put on the National Register. Then a local district was created around those buildings to protect the entire downtown commercial area through special zoning and special ordinances. That really started the thinking of revitalizing downtown."[12]

In the 1970s and 1980s, strip malls located outside of Sanford's historic downtown area lured shoppers and businesses away from the heart of the city, allowing the older buildings to survive impending development.

More than twenty historic buildings are extant in downtown Sanford, most of them dating from 1887. The architectural styles represented include neoclassical, Turkish, Romanesque revival, and Florentine palazzo. Because of local historic preservation efforts, the entire commercial district of Sanford will remain intact, offering visitors a unique look into Central Florida's past.[13]

Still standing in downtown Sanford is the DeForest Building, constructed in 1887. The DeForest Building is the only survivor of the 1887 fire in Sanford. Designed in the beaux-arts architectural style, the building has an elaborate cornice and segmental pediments over the windows. Alterations in 1917 and 1941 did not destroy the original detail of the building.

One of the most recently constructed buildings in Sanford's downtown historic district is the six-story skyscraper that opened in 1923 as the First National Bank. The bank was forced to close in 1929, but by 1938 another bank moved into the building. Since 1938 the building has continuously housed a series of banks.

A two-block area of Sanford's Magnolia Avenue, between First Street and Third Street, has been designated the Cultural Corridor. The Imperial Opera House, built in 1910, and the Ritz Theater, built in 1923, are both in the Cultural Corridor. The opera house remains boarded up and abandoned, but the Ritz Theater, where vaudeville shows were presented, is currently being renovated. Alicia Clark explains that, in the past, the Ritz Theater has

The Hotchkiss Building on First Street in Sanford is one of the town's oldest buildings. Constructed in the late 1880s, the Hotchkiss Building is an example of Romanesque revival architecture. Other architectural styles found in downtown Sanford include neoclassical, Turkish, and Florentine palazzo.

served as the center of community activity in Sanford: "The Ritz was built as the Milane Theater in the mid-1920s. It was built by a Mr. Miller and a Mr. Lane, who combined their names and called it the Milane, and then years later under another owner it became the Ritz. The Ritz was the center of town. When the World Series was played, it was broadcast into the street from the Ritz Theater, and the whole town would come down and listen to it. From the silent movie era on up through recent years, it was the movie house in town. It's not exactly a movie palace, but it's a large movie theater. It's somewhat unusual for this area because it still has the flies above the stage where backdrops can be raised and lowered, and it has large doors on the back of the stage where things can be brought in. The theater was meant to have Chautauqua programs and live performances in addition to movies, and that's what it's going back to."[14]

The Ritz Theater closed in the mid-1980s and was abandoned for more than a decade, creating an extensive restoration project. While the building was structurally sound, a leaking roof left standing water in the theater's orchestra pit and caused extensive interior damage.

Fred Rogers, co–executive director of the Historic Ritz Theater Project, plans for live productions to be staged at the Ritz Theater in the near future, explaining that the building requires extensive renovation first: "A lot of things need to be done. It needs restoration plastering. All of the theater seats have to be removed. We've discovered some of the original deco art-work, which we will document and have restored. It's got a beautiful color palette to it. We've retained one of the original light fixtures, and we're going to have them duplicated. I found out that there was a pipe organ in there at one time, and I want to investigate having a pipe organ put back in. There's a lovely balcony space. One feature of the theater that I find quite significant is it retains the original segregated entrance for the black popu-lation. The side door, the original drinking fountain, the original entrance, and the original restroom are still intact, and I feel that's a historically sig-nificant feature which we need to preserve also."[15]

Next door to the Ritz Theater in Sanford's Cultural Corridor is the First Street Gallery. The building, constructed in 1919, is now an exhibition space for visual art, but in the past it has housed an A&P Food Store, a garage, a bookstore, a real estate office, a Florida Power and Light office, and a dis-count carpet store.

Kay Bartholomew, owner of the First Street Gallery and also co–execu-tive director of the Historic Ritz Theater Project, is helping to renovate the theater as she refurbishes her gallery next door. Bartholomew says that the historic preservation efforts underway in Sanford are attracting artists and young professionals to the town, and she explains why she chose to open an art gallery in an old building in desperate need of repair: "Well, for one thing, it had been designated a cultural center, the two blocks here, and that fit in very well with what we were trying to accomplish from an economic development standpoint, as well as a preservation standpoint. I'd had a gal-lery down on First Street, so we just moved it up here, and we kept the name because it had been established. I think it had more interest because it is an old building. It's not a historically significant building, but it had possibilities on the interior, particularly, for a gallery. Then adding the pres-ence of the Ritz Theater really gave it a double meaning, and I think it's exciting, fun, and challenging."[16]

In addition to serving as a space for visual art exhibitions, the First Street

The Ritz Theater, built in 1923, is currently being restored. The First Street Gallery is located in the building next door, which was built in 1919. The Ritz Theater is located in Sanford's Cultural Corridor, which also includes the Imperial Opera House, constructed in 1910.

Gallery is doubling as a theater space until the renovations at the Ritz Theater are completed. Funds raised from the performances at the First Street Gallery go toward the restoration of the Ritz Theater.

As historic buildings are being preserved in Sanford's commercial district, efforts are also under way to revitalize historic homes in the town. The Sanford Historic Trust was established in 1989 to preserve and beautify the homes in the residential historic district. The group presents several fundraisers a year, including a tour of historic homes, held the first weekend in December. Money raised by the Sanford Historic Trust is dispersed through grants. Individual homeowners are provided with funds for paint and other renovation supplies, and community restoration projects on public structures in the residential district are also sponsored.

Karen Ratliff-McNeil, president of the Sanford Historic Trust, emphasizes the diversity of historic homes in Sanford: "Sanford has one of the widest variety of home styles in all of Florida. We have over thirteen historic home styles. Anywhere from late Victorian, to arts and crafts, to Sears home kits, and they range from small bungalows, which predominate in the district, to some very large Victorian homes. The oldest one is from about 1880, and they are still in good repair, and are still occupied. The historic district is quite beautiful because of our canopy of trees. We have over forty-eight hundred trees on the rights of way, not including those in the yards."[17]

Together, the residential and commercial historic districts in Sanford provide both visitors and people living in Central Florida with a unique opportunity to see what a local town looked like in the late nineteenth and early twentieth centuries.

Historic preservation efforts are often misperceived as trying to limit progress and growth. The preservation efforts underway in Sanford are a prime example of how a community can be economically revitalized by retaining a unique character, which encourages cultural tourism and attracts new residents. While the Zora Neale Hurston Festival of the Arts and Humanities is the best example of how the history of Central Florida can be celebrated through an active cultural event, the town of Sanford stands apart as the most physically well preserved city in the region.

The old Fire Station in Sanford has been fully restored into a private residence and artist's studio. The town's downtown historic district is adjacent to the residential historic district, which contains many houses listed on the National Register of Historic Homes.

✸ Kissimmee

Cowboy Culture and Hispanic Traditions

The town of Kissimmee is best known as the neighbor of Disney World. Tourists and residents in Central Florida are familiar with the Highway 192 corridor, a seemingly endless series of hotels, T-shirt shops, and restaurants that present themed shows. Behind the neon and chaser-lights of Highway 192 is one of the oldest communities in the region, a town that preserves its historic traditions. The very name *Kissimmee* pays homage to the area's earliest inhabitants: it is an Anglicized version of the Caloosa Indian word *Cacema*.[1] The meaning of the word is forgotten.

What is remembered in Kissimmee is the town's history as an important contributor to Florida's cattle industry. While tourism is now the primary source of income for Kissimmee, the cattle industry is alive and well. Many active ranches still exist, and the cowboy culture is celebrated annually with the Silver Spurs Rodeo and the Kissimmee Bluegrass Festival.

The fastest-growing segment of Kissimmee's population is Hispanic. Latin people from Central America, South America, Cuba, Puerto Rico, and other Latin countries are moving to Kissimmee in large numbers. The Viva Osceola Festival and other events sponsored by the Osceola Center for the Arts celebrate Hispanic traditions. Although Spanish-speaking people were not the first to establish a permanent settlement in the Kissimmee area, they were the first to bring cattle to the region.

After "discovering" Florida in 1513, Ponce de León returned eight years later to establish a colony. Attacks by the Caloosa Indians forced Ponce de Leon to leave, abandoning a herd of Andalusian cattle. Those animals are believed to be the first domesticated cattle to be brought to North America.[2] When the Spanish explorer Hernando de Soto came to Southwest Florida in 1539, he also brought herds of cattle with him. As de Soto moved north through the center of the state, it is believed that many of the cows strayed and were left behind.[3] Native Americans living in the area that would become Kissimmee domesticated and bred some of the cows, while others roamed free. As white settlers came to the region in the 1840s, establishing a cattle industry seemed prudent.

Selling cattle was the Kissimmee area's only source of income for about forty years. During the Civil War the local cattle industry boomed. Under the direction of Jacob Summerlin, the "King of the Crackers," Central Florida cattle became the primary source of food for the Confederate Army.[4] Many of the families active in Kissimmee's cattle business today can trace their roots back to men who raised cattle during the Civil War, such as Jack Yates, Henry Overstreet, George W. Bronson, and Isaac Lanier.

The Lanier Homestead, from the early 1900s, is protected by the Osceola County Historical Society. The Lanier family still lives in the Kissimmee area. The Lanier Homestead was moved to its present location by truck from western Osceola County and furnished with period antiques.

Following the Civil War, African American families began participating in the local cattle industry. Tom Silas was one of the first successful black cowmen in Kissimmee. When he died, Silas owned several thousand acres of land and two thousand head of cattle. Unfortunately, the lack of a will made it impossible for Silas's wife and children to hold on to the estate. Lawrence Silas, the son of Tom Silas, eventually rebuilt the family cattle business into an even bigger operation than his father had owned.[5]

The railroad came to Kissimmee in 1882, expanding tourism, citrus farming, and cattle exportation. During the late 1880s through the early 1900s, steamboat traffic on the Kissimmee River also aided local industry. In the early part of the twentieth century, Kissimmee cattlemen overcame livestock parasites such as stomach worms and the Texas fever tick. The ranchers successfully bred their Spanish cow descendants with Brahman, Angus, and Hereford stock.[6]

In 1934 the Florida Cattlemen's Association was formed in Kissimmee. The group addresses local cattle-industry concerns such as promoting the sale of Florida-grown meat and fighting adverse legislation. In 1938 the Kissimmee Livestock Auction Market was established to sell cattle on a weekly basis. An arena was constructed next to the Auction Market, where the first Silver Spurs Rodeo was held in 1944.[7]

It was estimated that about one thousand people attended the first Silver Spurs Rodeo; the improved facility used today holds ten thousand. The traditions of performing the Quadrille on Horseback and other rodeo skills are passed from one generation to the next in Kissimmee.[8] David Snedeker, president of the Osceola County Historical Society, explains the importance of the Silver Spurs Rodeo to Kissimmee residents: "The Silver Spurs Rodeo started in the '40s and is the main event in the community. As a matter of fact, Osceola County schools still get a day off for the rodeo—'Rodeo Day'—that I'm sure other counties don't recognize as an official holiday day off. Rodeo Day was scheduled for children to be off because they had involvement in the cattle industry; they participated in the County Fair, and the rodeo was the main community event for a long, long time. Tourism has surpassed the cattle industry, but it's still a major industry. Much of the county is still mainly cattle ranches."[9]

Music has always been an important part of the cowboy culture that developed in Kissimmee. The ranchers and their families entertained themselves with bluegrass, a type of country music performed on acoustic string instruments such as banjo, fiddle, guitar, and mandolin. Bluegrass music is also characterized by the use of free improvisation and close vocal harmonies.[10] Ranchers gathering at the Silver Spurs Rodeo and the Kissimmee Livestock Auction Market staged impromptu musical performances.

In 1977 the Kiwanis Club of Kissimmee organized a more formal celebration of cowboy-culture music, the Kissimmee Bluegrass Festival. The annual event is held on the Silver Spurs Rodeo grounds in early March. More than six thousand people attend the three-day festival, many staying in campers or recreational vehicles. Nationally known performers such as the Lewis Family, the Osborne Brothers, Eddie Adcock, and IIIrd Tyme Out play the Kissimmee Bluegrass Festival, as well as regional and local musicians. The Kiwanis Club donates proceeds from the event to local charities and to a college scholarship fund.

The explosion of tourist-oriented businesses in Kissimmee has not deterred the efforts of those interested in the physical preservation of historic buildings. The offices of the Osceola County Historical Society are located less than a quarter of a mile from the Highway 192 corridor, where the organization has preserved two historic structures.

David Snedeker has seen the rapid growth of Kissimmee and works to preserve the historic culture of the town. He explains: "I came to Kissimmee in 1958, and I remember when 192 was a two-lane country road. There's been a lot of change since that time, and it continues to grow. In order to progress, you need to know about your past. Kissimmee and Osceola County have a colorful past. The Historical Society moved to this location in the mid-'80s. In the process of doing that and acquiring enough property to set up some larger exhibits, two homesteads were moved here. The first one, the main one, is the Lanier Homestead, which came from western Osceola County. It's a home from the early 1900s that was moved here by truck and furnished with period antiques. The other house is the Tyson House. It's a little bit smaller than the Lanier Homestead, and it was moved here and set up as a Country Store from the turn of the century."[11]

The Osceola County Historical Society was formed in 1949 and has accumulated many artifacts from the 1800s and early 1900s, which are dis-

The Tyson House, built in the late 1800s, is maintained as a country store by the Osceola County Historical Society. In addition to keeping the Tyson House and the Lanier Homestead open to the public, the Osceola County Historical Society collects local antiques and artifacts and is actively involved in the preservation of historic buildings throughout Kissimmee.

played in a building near the Tyson House. In addition to making the two homesteads and local antiques accessible to the public, the society is interested in the preservation of other historic buildings in Kissimmee.

The Osceola County Courthouse was completed in 1890, three years after Osceola County was created from portions of Orange and Brevard Counties. The oldest courthouse in Florida in continuous use, the Osceola County Courthouse is a three-story red-brick building. Typical of Romanesque revival courthouses constructed throughout the United States during the late 1800s, the building is one of four remaining in Florida.[12] The Romanesque architectural elements of the courthouse include the tower above the entrance, the round arches on the portico and above the doors, and the segmental arches above the windows.

The original Osceola High School was built in 1925 and was used as an educational institution until 1964. The Mediterranean-revival building is an example of the Spanish-influenced architecture popular in Florida in the 1920s. The structure is currently used as a storage facility for the Osceola County School Board.

The Osceola County Courthouse, built in 1890, is the oldest Florida courthouse in continuous use. The building is typical of Romanesque revival courthouses constructed throughout the United States in the late 1800s, but is one of only four remaining in Florida.

The Holy Redeemer Catholic Church, constructed in 1912, was one of the first Catholic churches in Central Florida. Located on West Sproule Avenue in Kissimmee, the church is now a Methodist chapel. The First United Methodist Church, located on North Church Street, was built in 1913. The red-brick building retains its original character, although new wings and classrooms have been added to it.

Completed in 1968, the Osceola Center for the Arts is not yet an historic building, but it is a primary location of cultural events in Kissimmee.[13] The original home of the Osceola County Historical Society, the center now houses a theater, a music hall, and two art galleries. Performances ranging from community theater productions to symphonic concerts are presented at the center, and work by a variety of local, national, and international visual artists is displayed there. The Osceola Center for the Arts also sponsors a series of events designed to preserve the traditions of Kissimmee's expanding Latin population.

Many Anglo-Americans in Central Florida recognize the value of learning about Latin culture and welcome opportunities to expand their understanding of and appreciation for Hispanic art, music, dance, and food. Peter Edwards is not Hispanic, but as executive director of the Osceola Center for the Arts he founded the Viva Osceola Festival in 1992. Edwards wanted to create an authentic Latin festival that would both serve the growing Latin population of Central Florida and introduce other members of the community to the culture of their neighbors. He explains: "The Arts Center has been involved in trying to establish a number of new cultural events in the community, and we recognized that there had been such a massive growth in this area of Latin people that we felt it was important that we get involved in that. For example, since the mid-'80s the population in Osceola County has grown from less than six percent Hispanic to nearly twenty percent in ten years. So we started a festival to serve that segment of our community. The first two years were kind of small. We involved some members from the Latin community and sort of felt our way. It's designed to be a cultural event, and as more members of the community, particularly the Latin community, have recognized that we're doing this for them, more of them are taking an active interest in it."[14]

In an effort to further involve the Latin community in the Viva Osceola Festival, Edwards hired an Hispanic special events coordinator in 1994 to help organize the event. Angie del Riego Maloney moved to Central Florida from the Dominican Republic and has had a significant impact on the success of the Viva Osceola Festival, attracting thousands of people to the event. Rather than exclusively bringing in musicians and artists from outside of Central Florida to participate in the festival, Maloney employs local performers and artists. The locally popular musical groups Sol Latino, Trapiche, and Mariache Cobre have performed at the Viva Osceola Festival, as well as flamenco dancer Rachael Tacon, and various folkloric dance groups from Central Florida.

Maloney feels that using local performers at the Viva Osceola Festival galvanizes the Latin community: "It brings people together as a whole. There's a lot of Latins around here, a lot of Hispanics, but the Hispanic community is not very united. I feel that there is a need for unification in the Hispanic community and that the only way to do that unification is by using the music and the art and our culture. You have to maintain traditions because they are part of you. Traditions and where you come from you can never forget. You can never leave them behind because that's what gives you your identity as a person. Even if you go to a country and you spend a lifetime in another country that is not yours, you're always going to have your identity in where you came from and your roots. That's important for you to develop it and keep it and to pass it on to your kids, and their kids, and so on."[15]

In addition to organizing the Viva Osceola Festival, Maloney is an active participant as a singer and guitarist and as a visual artist who works primarily in charcoal and colored pencil, and also acrylic. To expand the cultural offerings of the festival, Maloney created an exhibition of Latin art to run concurrently with the event. In 1994 just three local artists, including Maloney, displayed their work in the exhibition, but now it attracts dozens of submissions from Hispanic artists across the state. Maloney explains why she named the annual exhibition "Matices": "*Matices* means hues of the same color, and what it signifies is the races, the mix of races from Latin countries. There is many Latin countries, there's South America, there's Central America, there's the Caribbean, and each of us is distinctive, each of us is different in our own way. Even though there is so many races mixed in, we have a lot of things in common. Our art is the same, we come from the same background almost, we've had the same problems through the years. We struggle the same way, we are mostly sub-developed countries that are struggling. We have that in common. Our music is similar too, so we have a lot of things in common."[16]

Much of the artwork displayed at the Matices exhibitions focuses on political oppression and poor living conditions in Latin countries. The art also expresses fond memories of native countries still thought of as home. The Matices exhibition is a complement to the live performances, craft displays, and Latin food offerings at the Viva Osceola Festival.

While the Viva Osceola Festival is intended to be a cultural celebration for Hispanic people, Maloney hopes that it also serves as a way for other Central Floridians to become familiar with and enjoy Latin culture: "It's not a festival designed for Latin people only. It's a festival designed to show Latin culture to the other culture and let them see what we're about so that we can somehow cross the border and come to understand each other better. We are doing the presentations by the master of ceremonies in English. Even though all of the songs and all of the entertainment is going to be in

The Osceola Center for the Arts, which presents the Viva Osceola Festival, is housed in this building, which includes a theater, a music hall, and two art galleries. The 1968 building was originally the home of the Osceola County Historical Society. The Osceola Center for the Arts serves as a venue for local performing and visual artists.

Spanish, the presentations by the master of ceremonies will be in English so that the Anglo-American people can enjoy it as well. They can understand at least what's going on and understand where this music comes from, why they sing it this way, some of the history of Latin music and culture." [17]

As special events coordinator at the Osceola Center for the Arts, Maloney has also created a Latin Christmas celebration to preserve Hispanic holiday traditions in Kissimmee. The annual event combines performances of traditional music with theatrical scenes of typical Christmas celebrations in Latin countries. Most of the dialogue is in English, allowing non-Hispanic members of the community to learn more about Latin culture.

The preservation of Latin traditions in Kissimmee through the Viva Osceola Festival, the Matices exhibition, and the Latin Christmas program provides an interesting complement to the celebrations of cowboy culture at the Silver Spurs Rodeo and the Kissimmee Bluegrass Festival. Hispanic people made the cattle industry possible in Kissimmee by bringing livestock to the area in the 1500s. Both cowboy heritage and Hispanic traditions are important elements of the tourism-dominated culture in modern Kissimmee.

✸ Mount Dora

A Look Back in Time

U.S. Highway 441 enters Florida from Fargo, Georgia, passes by the Osceola National Forest, and essentially winds through the center of the state. The road runs through Gainesville, past the University of Florida, and into the heart of many small towns. The highest concentration of topless bars and adult stores in the city of Orlando can be found along a brief stretch of the highway. In South Florida, 441 takes the traveler along the shore of Lake Okeechobee before heading east by the Arthur R. Marshall National Wildlife Reserve, then south again, parallel to the coast.

In Central Florida's Lake County, U.S. Highway 441 was originally going to pass through Mount Dora after leaving Tavares on the way to Zellwood and Apopka. Instead, the road makes a curve around Mount Dora, allowing the town's nearly eight thousand year-round residents and many visitors to enjoy the ambience of a bygone era. Early-twentieth-century lamp-posts line the road leading to Mount Dora's downtown, which has only two stoplights. Historic homes and buildings, none more than two stories high, stand well preserved, housing dozens of antique and specialty shops, restaurants, and art galleries. Donnelly Park, with its busy shuffleboard and tennis courts, takes up a block of the downtown area. Two lakeside parks within walking distance of downtown Mount Dora feature a picnic area, a playground, a nature walk, a boat ramp, and a small lighthouse.

The quaint town of Mount Dora hosts a well-respected annual outdoor art festival, as well as frequent antique and craft fairs, antique boat and auto shows, and historic home tours. The Mount Dora Center for the Arts presents new work by Florida artists, and in the alley directly behind it, the Royellou Museum displays photographs and artifacts from Mount Dora's past. Concerts of classical music and jazz are often presented, and the Mount Dora Theater Company stages a full season of musicals and plays.

As chairman of the Mount Dora Historic Preservation Committee and a board member of the Mount Dora Historical Society, David Phelps is active in efforts to maintain and restore the cultural heritage of the town. Phelps says that if U.S. Highway 441 had been built through Mount Dora as the original plans called for, the impact would have been devastating: "The entire town wouldn't even be here. Mr. Dick Edgerton, the guy who was responsible for 441 bypassing the city, is awful modest about it and won't comment on how important it is, but that's the only reason Mount Dora is here. Unlike other cities who wanted the new four-lane 441 to come right down through their town—I won't name any names, but they're urban blights now—Mount Dora for selfish reasons or whatever, not strictly preservation reasons at the time, they fought to have it routed out of the way, around the city. It loops around the city; a straight line would have been through town. Because of that one simple thing, which took a lot of what Mr. Edgerton likes to refer to as 'unelective politics,' behind the scenes in Tallahassee, because certain landowners and the majority of business owners wanted it to go through town, because in the short term it would have made a lot of money, but that is the main key thing, why we have Mount Dora the way it is today. Because of the rerouting of the road."[1]

The first group of people known to have lived in the Mount Dora area, excluding Native Americans, is the Drawdy family. The Drawdys' homestead is two miles south of what is now Mount Dora. When surveyors hired by the United States government came to Central Florida in the 1850s to map the area's rivers, lakes, and terrain, Dora Ann Drawdy was so kind to them that they named the largest lake in the vicinity Lake Dora.[2]

Other early settlers are known to have lived in the area, but, as David Phelps explains, any records of who they were have been lost: "There was a skip in development between like 1845 and '50 to 1870. What happened— well, it happened in a lot of Florida, because of the Civil War. Florida just about dried up on the vine, and there were no settlers. There were other people around Mount Dora early on, besides the Drawdys. We don't know who they were. When the early settlers came here—the settlers that ended up officially, legally homesteading came here—they found other people living here that were squatters. Some moved on, some of them paid a few hundred dollars for their rights, so those people we'll never know who they are. There's the big space of time there from when the first settlement occurred in Florida, which was when the Indians were conquered, until the Civil War, and then it was put off until around the 1870s, and a lot of people moved here for a new start from other parts of the South, and from up North. It was like the frontier, just like out west. A lot of Westerns you see on television could really be Southerns because the same thing happened down here."[3]

In 1874 the Simpson family became the first people to homestead in what is now Mount Dora, and gradually other families joined them. Movement into the Lake Dora region was made much easier when a railroad came to nearby Fort Mason in 1880. In the summer of 1880, the local residents petitioned the U.S. Post Office Department to provide them with mail service, and they appointed Ross C. Tremain postmaster. Both Simpson and Tremain descendants still live in Mount Dora.

To receive mail, the town needed a name, so Mrs. I. M. Mabbette suggested *Royellou*, a combination of *Roy*, *Ella*, and *Lou*, the names of Tremain's three children.[4] The name was adopted by the town, but only for a few years. No one is certain exactly when Royellou's name was changed to Mount Dora, but evidence exists that the date was in the summer of 1882. Dr. C. R. Gilbert came to Mount Dora on December 18, 1882, and wrote in his diary that Mount Dora was "now an infant town, only four months old."[5]

In 1882 the first school was established in Mount Dora to serve the sixteen families in the town. The following year an historic building that is still in use today was built, bringing a steady influx of vacationers to Mount Dora to enjoy mild winter weather, bird-watching, hunting, fishing, boating, and lawn bowling.

The Lakeside Inn was built by Civil War Colonel James M. Alexander, John P. Donnelly, and Colonel John A. MacDonald. Open only during the winter months, the inn had ten rooms and was called the Alexander House.

Ten years after it was constructed, in 1893, Alexander, Donnelly, and Mac-Donald sold the Alexander House to Emma Boone, and she changed the name of the hotel to the Lake House. In 1903 Boone married George D. Thayer, and together they greatly expanded what is now the Lakeside Inn. A gatehouse, the three-story main building, a dining room, and a kitchen area were all constructed by the Thayers in the early 1900s, paving the way for the hotel's heyday.[6]

Bill West, president of the Mount Dora Historical Society, explains why the Lakeside Inn was so important to the development of the town: "It had a lot to do with the building up of Mount Dora and the tourist business. In the late 1890s they had a lot of freezes. Everyone lost all of their orange groves, or whatever they were growing, and most of them left. There were not many people left in this area. Then in the 1920s, when the big land boom started, people started coming down by trains. They were faster, and they had rails all over the place by then, so you could go pretty direct. People started coming down from up north and building homes, and that's also when we started having a big tourist influx. In 1930 President Calvin Coolidge and his wife came to the Lakeside Inn. We have an old photograph of when they were here, the Coolidges, and they planted a tree in front of our community building. There are a lot of people who still live here who are in that photograph. They're a little bit older, but they're still here. We even have the shovel they used."[7]

By 1887 Mount Dora had its own railroad station across the street from the Lakeside Inn, and by 1915 there were two passenger trains a day arriving there from each direction. The steady railroad traffic helped provide business for the hotel and for Mount Dora. Today the old railroad station is preserved as the home of the Mount Dora Chamber of Commerce.

In 1924 the Edgerton family bought the Lakeside Inn and managed it until 1980. In 1984 the management group that now owns the inn spent nearly $4 million restoring the buildings to their original condition. Today the Lakeside Inn looks just as it did in photographs taken in the 1920s and 1930s. The Lakeside Inn is listed on the National Register of Historic Places and is one of only five Florida hotels named an Historic Hotel of America by the Trust for Historic Preservation.

A three-mile walking tour of Mount Dora, facilitated by a map provided

One of a group of buildings that comprise Mount Dora's historic Lakeside Inn. Originally called the Alexander House, the hotel was built by Civil War Colonel James M. Alexander, John P. Donnelly, and Colonel John A. MacDonald. The Lakeside Inn is listed on the National Register of Historic Places and is one of only five Florida hotels named an Historic Hotel of America by the Trust for Historic Preservation.

by the Chamber of Commerce, allows the visitor to see thirty historic homes, buildings, and sites. The oldest homes date from the early 1880s, and the newest structures were built in the late 1920s. Included on the tour are the Colonel Alexander House, the former home of the owner of Mount Dora's first general store, and the Community Congregational Church, built in 1887. The Donnelly House, built in 1893, survives as one of the only examples of steamboat-Gothic architecture in the state and has served as the Masonic Temple Lodge since 1930. The Watt House was used by the original owner in the early 1900s to box oranges for shipment and is currently the home of the great-granddaughter of Mount Dora's first homesteader. The architectural styles found in Mount Dora range from basic farmhouses with wraparound porches to ornate gingerbread houses.

The Royellou Museum is unique because of its location in the old city jail and fire station. Exhibits of historic photographs, documents, artifacts, and memorabilia are shown in the tiny cells of the jail, which still have

The Donnelly House, built in 1893, is one of the only examples of steamboat-Gothic architecture in Florida. This unique building has served as the Masonic Temple Lodge since 1930. The Donnelly House is one of thirty historic homes, buildings, and sites in Mount Dora.

metal-barred doors. Mount Dora Historical Society President Bill West explains the origin of the building, which was built following a fire in the early 1920s that destroyed much of the town: "It was built in 1922, right after the big fire. Right after the big fire they decided they needed a fire department, which is a good idea, but it's too bad they didn't think of it beforehand. Mr. J. P. Donnelly had this piece of property in one of the alleyways [which] he donated to the city of Mount Dora [provided] the city would build a fire house and a little jail. So they built this building out of block, just plain old cement block. They put in six cells, very small, and no facilities—no water, no sewers, nothing—you just had one of those little pots. And they built a little room off of it that's maybe fifteen by twenty, and they bought a hand pumper, that you had to pull around town by hand, you couldn't even use a horse, and that's how they kept fires under control. They had a bell to notify volunteers, and they'd all run down there, get out the hand pumper, and they'd run five blocks up the hill, and by the time they got up to the top of the hill, they could wet down the ashes."[8]

While historic preservation has become important to the residents of Mount Dora, they are not living in the past. Almost every weekend there is a festival or performing-arts event in the town. In early February the annual Mount Dora Art Festival is held in Donnelly Park, attracting hundreds of artists from across the country. The art festival is sponsored by the Mount Dora Center for the Arts, which continually exhibits work by Florida artists. Several times a year an Antique Extravaganza is held, hosted by Renniger's Twin Markets, the town's largest antique dealer. In late October the annual Craft Fair is held downtown. Antique boat shows, antique car shows, and an annual bicycle festival are all popular events in Mount Dora.

The major performing arts group in Lake County is the Mount Dora Theater Company, a community theater that has been active since 1948. Until the summer of 1997, the Mount Dora Theater Company was known as the Icehouse Theater. The theater originally was located downtown in a converted icehouse—hence the name. Although the theater company relo-

The Community Congregational Church, constructed in 1887, is Mount Dora's oldest church and one of the town's oldest buildings. The church survived a fire in the early 1920s that destroyed much of downtown Mount Dora. In 1922 a combination fire station and city jail was built, which now houses the Royellou Museum.

cated to a larger space just outside of the downtown area, it retained the unusual moniker for half a century.[9] The theater's productions are well attended and usually receive positive reviews from regional critics.

Mount Dora's three parks are often the sites of outdoor concerts sponsored by the city. A nature walk in Palm Island Park has a boardwalk for viewing the wildlife living in and around Lake Dora. Despite the town's name, do not expect to go mountain hiking in Mount Dora. Although the town's elevation of 184 feet above sea level officially makes it a "mount," the area's hills slope very gently. Central Florida is almost entirely flat and even small hills are unusual. A popular bumper sticker jokes, "I Climbed Mount Dora."

While historic preservation is now popular in Mount Dora, that has not always been the case. Many important buildings have been lost. As chairman of the Mount Dora Historic Preservation Committee, David Phelps believes preservation efforts are essential for the town to maintain a sense of community: "Historic preservation certainly helps tourism. Tourists love it, but I'm more interested in the people that live here, the citizens, to have a feeling of where they live and a feeling of the past, a sense of place, a sense of community. If you slowly knock down all the buildings, you're not going to have that. There's been a lot of studies—psychological studies—made, and when you take people out of their environment and put them in another environment where things are sterile and nothing is familiar, a lot of strange things happen to people. A lot of crime is attributed to that, because they don't have that anchoring feeling that you get from seeing familiar things around you, and seeing landmarks."[10]

Phelps laments the loss of several old homes that were torn down to create parking lots, but he believes the residents of Mount Dora have become aware of the value of preserving the past. As property values in the area rise, Phelps fears greed may result in the loss of more historic buildings to make way for apartment buildings or department stores. For now though, Mount Dora stands as a reminder of what life was like in Central Florida in the late nineteenth and early twentieth centuries and is an important example of our cultural heritage.

❀ DeLand

The Athens of Florida

Many historic buildings from the late nineteenth and early twentieth centuries still stand in both Sanford and Mount Dora. Significant portions of both towns allow the visitor to see the variety of architectural styles used by the first permanent residents of Central Florida, and museums in both towns preserve images and artifacts from the past for future generations. Similarly, residents of DeLand, in Volusia County, have active historic preservation efforts under way to protect the character and ambience of their town from encroaching urban sprawl.

While the original appearance of many of the buildings in the downtown area of Sanford is essentially maintained today, most of the historic buildings in Mount Dora and DeLand have been renovated using bright, modern colors of paint, and eye-catching awnings hang over the entrances to most businesses. Comparisons can also be drawn between DeLand and the city of Winter Park, since both are college towns. Winter Park is totally surrounded by the greater Orlando area, however, while DeLand retains the feel of a small town.

DeLand is the home of Stetson University, Florida's oldest private institution of higher learning. The school, founded in 1883 (two years before Winter Park's Rollins College), is the center of activity in DeLand. Several of Stetson's main buildings are the originals constructed in the late 1800s. Elizabeth Hall, the focal point of the campus, has been the site of concerts, commencements, lectures, and chapel services for more than a century. A nine-hundred-seat auditorium in Elizabeth Hall houses a huge, elaborately ornamented pipe organ.

The several blocks that make up DeLand's downtown historic district are on one side of the Stetson campus, and the town's historic homes were also built near the school. While car dealerships, fast-food chains, and strip malls surround the heart of the town, DeLand's downtown area and the campus of Stetson have been well preserved.

Sallee Hardy, president of the West Volusia Historical Society, believes that historic preservation is what has allowed DeLand to retain a strong sense of community: "There's a charm about DeLand that has always been there. It didn't disappear with a lot of new buildings and a lot of malls coming along to close up shops on DeLand's main street, on the boulevard. There has been a year here and a year there where you had empty store-fronts, but on a whole, the Mainstreet Association has really seen that the boulevard has stayed nice small businesses. Part of it is the charm of having

Elizabeth Hall, the focal point of Stetson University, was named after hat manufacturer John B. Stetson's wife in 1889. Founded in 1883, Stetson University is Florida's oldest private institution of higher learning. A 900-seat auditorium in Elizabeth Hall houses a huge, elaborately ornamented pipe organ.

the university there. So many people that you talk to have come back. They'll say that they grew up in DeLand, went away and traveled, lived here, there, and everywhere, but they wanted to come back to that charming small-town feeling that they get. People that buy homes are really dedicated to preserving them and fixing them up. DeLand used to be the kind of town that when you walked down the sidewalk of the boulevard, you knew everyone. You would stop and talk and what have you. I would say when you look at it today, it still has that friendly atmosphere, which I think is very important. I think a great deal of that has to do with the willingness of people to preserve the buildings and their interest in history."[1]

The history of DeLand goes back to 1876, when businessman Henry A. DeLand came from his home in Fairport, New York, to visit his sister in Central Florida. DeLand's sister had married O. P. Terry, and they had a homestead in what was to become DeLand. Henry DeLand came to Central Florida by train to Jacksonville, took a steamship down the St Johns River to Enterprise, and from there took a horse and buggy to west Volusia County. He was so impressed with the beauty and climate of the area that he decided to start a town there.[2]

Mr. DeLand had made a fortune manufacturing baking soda in New York, and he proceeded to spend his money buying large tracts of land in Central Florida. To entice others to settle in his new town, he offered to buy back the land he sold from anyone who was unhappy living in his town. Van Rhodes, an active member of the West Volusia Historical Society, explains that DeLand's overconfidence and generosity led to his financial ruin: "The Big Freeze came in 1895, and wiped out all the citrus and other crops. DeLand's friends got disenchanted and wanted their money back. Well, it cost him his fortune to buy back the property, but before he died in 1908, he had made good to his word: he didn't owe anybody. Before that, the town grew very rapidly. He established the DeLand Academy, which later became Stetson University. He established a public school, which was also the meeting house for the churches, until each denomination built their own church facility. He brought in entertainers for cultural activities. He called this the 'Athens of Florida,' with its educational, cultural, religious connotation, and DeLand is still known as the 'Athens of Florida' today."[3]

One of DeLand's friends who contributed greatly to the development of the town was the famous hat manufacturer John B. Stetson. By 1889 Stetson had contributed so much time and money to the development of the DeLand Academy that the name of the institution was changed to Stetson University. Elizabeth Hall, the focal point of the school, was named after Stetson's wife.[4]

Like its neighbors Sanford and Mount Dora, the town of DeLand lost many of its original buildings to a destructive fire.[5] Following the 1886 blaze, the town of DeLand passed an ordinance that allowed only brick buildings to be constructed in the commercial district, which makes preservation efforts today much easier. Many wooden homes that survived the 1886 fire still stand in DeLand.

The DeLand House Museum serves as the headquarters of the West Volusia Historical Society, which makes historical documents, photographs, and memorabilia available to researchers. With the exception of a modern office

Stetson University's DeLand Hall was the first building constructed on the campus and is the oldest building in Florida continuously used for higher education. Originally called the DeLand Academy, the school's name was changed to Stetson University in 1889 to honor patron John B. Stetson.

upstairs, the DeLand House Museum is furnished as it might have been in the late 1800s, and local artifacts are displayed throughout the house. The West Volusia Historical Society presents an annual tour of historic DeLand homes during the first weekend in December, and in October celebrates the birthday of Henry A. DeLand by having an actor portray the town's founder.

The DeLand House Museum was originally the home of A. G. Hamlin, who bought the property from Henry A. DeLand. Hamlin was DeLand's first attorney and the developer of the Hamlin orange.[6] Hamlin's orange grove was located next to his house, which was built in 1886. The seedless, smooth-skinned Hamlin orange developed there is still a popular orange for both juice and eating.[7] When Hamlin first built what is now the DeLand House Museum, it was a 1½-story structure.

John B. Stetson bought the house from Hamlin in 1893, to serve as faculty housing for instructors at Stetson University. Ten years later Charles Farriss, a professor of Greek at Stetson, bought the home and made signifi-

George Hamlin, who developed the Hamlin orange, built this house in 1886. It is now the DeLand House Museum and home of the West Volusia Historical Society. The house is furnished as it might have been in the late 1800s, and historical documents, photographs, and memorabilia are stored in a modern office upstairs.

cant alterations. Farriss raised the roof of the house, making it a two-story structure, and relocated the staircase. A full-height Greek-revival portico was added to the east side of the house, and an entry porch was built on the south side. Farriss enjoyed working with stained glass and leaded glass, and his work can be seen around the doors of the home, over the fireplace, and on some of the cabinet doors.

Over the years the DeLand House Museum changed ownership several times, and in the 1940s it was converted into an apartment house. In 1988 the home was purchased by Robert and Hawtense Conrad and donated to the town. The DeLand House Museum was opened in 1990, after being restored to the condition it was in when Farriss lived there. The DeLand House Museum is a valuable resource for those who wish to explore late-nineteenth-century life in Central Florida.

The most recent historic preservation efforts underway in DeLand are focused on the Athens Theater. Built in 1921, the Athens Theater served as the cultural center of downtown DeLand in the early twentieth century. The Athens Theater was constructed by L. M. Patterson of Washington, D.C., who formed the DeLand Amusement Company.[8] Patterson hired Orlando architect Murray King to design the Athens Theater, which has a distinctive Italian Renaissance facade. Architectural details of the building include red tapestry brick contrasting with a cast concrete and terra-cotta dropped cornice, belt courses, shields, and curvilinear parapets.

The Athens Theater was modernized in 1950 by the Florida State Theaters chain. The alterations included installing air-conditioning and a new marquee and redesigning the lobby and auditorium. The Athens Theater became a movie house after being a venue for live theater and was later used as a dinner theater. Today the Mainstreet DeLand Association is working to have the Athens Theater restored to its original grandeur, to be used as a multipurpose arts facility.[9]

A variety of stimulating performing and visual art experiences add to the cultural life of DeLand. The students and faculty of Stetson University present frequent concerts, theatrical performances, and art exhibitions. The International Guitar Workshop is held every summer at Stetson, with performances open to the public. The American Guild of Organists, a national organization dedicated to organ and choral music, is based in DeLand. The

The Athens Theater, built in 1921, is currently being restored to its original condition. The theater was the cultural center of downtown DeLand in the early twentieth century. Architectural details of the building include a distinctive Italian Renaissance facade, red tapestry brick contrasting with a cast concrete and terra-cotta dropped cornice, belt courses, shields, and curvilinear parapets.

DeLand Fall Festival of the Arts, an outdoor art show, is held annually in November.

In the early 1990s the Cultural Arts Center, the home of the Storybook Theater Company and the DeLand Museum of Art, was constructed across from Stetson University. Workshops and classes in the visual and performing arts are offered to all age groups. Local historian Bill Dreggors frequently presents slide shows and lectures there that examine DeLand history.

Michael Sanden, executive director of the DeLand Museum of Art, points out that an important part of cultural preservation is collecting the work of local artists today, for future generations to enjoy: "This community is an absolute gem. Many people know it as a small, beautiful, historic area, but there are many people who are both from the DeLand area and also who have moved here, who have a strong bent on support of the arts, and history, and culture, music, and what-have-you. My vision is to take this museum and to focus its collections and focus its programs in several ways. Florida is now the fourth largest population state in the country, with certainly a wealth of artists and arts programs that exist. Many of the artists, many of the collections themselves, whether they happen to be private collections, corporate, or collections that are coming into the art museums and art centers, literally did not exist in the 1960s. I think it makes perfect sense to look at building a small but focused collection on the very best of the artists from our state."[10] Sanden realizes that the local art created in the present will be a part of our cultural heritage in the future and needs to be collected and preserved.

The Cultural Arts Center and the DeLand House Museum stimulate a sense of community in DeLand, while the presence of Stetson University earns the town a prominent place in Florida history. The active preservation of historic buildings and a wide variety of art exhibits, musical events, and theatrical performances combine to make DeLand a focal point of culture in Central Florida.

❋ Cassadaga

A Unique Religious Settlement

Any survey of the cultural heritage of Central Florida with an emphasis on how history is actively being used today to encourage a sense of community would be incomplete without a look at the village of Cassadaga and its inhabitants. Since 1894 the tiny town of Cassadaga has been a close-knit community known around the world as a home for the religion, philosophy, and science of Spiritualism. Cassadaga is recognized as the oldest active religious community in the southeastern United States and is designated an historic district on the National Register of Historic Places.

While most people today believe in life after death, they tend to remain skeptical about the abilities of self-proclaimed mediums. The philosophy of Spiritualism is centered around the belief that life continues after physical death and that mediums can be used to communicate with those who have passed on to the Spirit World. While many popular religions accept the divine revelations experienced by individuals, the religion of Spiritualism has empirical evidence to support the claim of communication with those no longer living in the physical world. Unlike most organized religions, Spiritualism does not ask its members for blind faith, but offers proof of its claims through individual readings that are overwhelmingly accurate, and by conducting healings of pathologic conditions that defy medical explanation.

Although Spiritualism is still widely practiced in Great Britain, its popularity has declined in the United States in the twentieth century. The tenets of Spiritualism were widely accepted in nineteenth-century America, but the fraudulent practice of mediumship and spiritual healings by unqualified people led to a mistrust of Spiritualism as a whole.[1]

Kristin Congdon, a professor of art at the University of Central Florida, is among a group of scholars assembled by photographer Gary Monroe, a professor at Daytona Beach Community College, to write a text to accompany a photojournalistic look at Cassadaga. Congdon's role in the Cassadaga Project is to collect oral narratives of the residents of and visitors to Cassadaga, and to examine the village's material culture spaces. She says that despite efforts by the Cassadaga Association to maintain the legitimacy of Spiritualism, misconceptions about the religion are still prevalent: "Because there was a lot of fakery going on at the turn of the century, a lot of Spiritualists were closed down. Now in places like Cassadaga, they monitor all of that very carefully and are very concerned about the kinds of people who do readings, who do spiritual counseling, and who address the public, so there isn't any fakery or forgery. A lot of the people who come here don't want to tell anyone else that they come here, or that they are Spiritualists. There is fear of losing their jobs, there is fear of reprisal. Many people who come here come initially out of curiosity; they want to see what it's all about. Some people feel standoffish about it like it's a place for witches, or Satanism. There are stories like 'birds don't fly over Cassadaga,' which of course they do. A lot of people come here on Halloween because they think that these people are doing strange kinds of rituals, and just foreign sorts of things. But when you really start paying attention to what the religion is all about, it really isn't so farfetched at all."[2]

Like most prejudice against a specific group of people, misconceptions about the residents of Cassadaga are born out of ignorance and fear by those who have no direct experience with that which they condemn. To the dismay of the Spiritualists of Cassadaga, groups of tarot-card readers, palm readers, unapproved mediums, fortune-tellers, and other psychics have established places of business directly across the street from the entrance to the village, adding fuel to public confusion about legitimate Spiritualism.[3]

Spiritualists believe in God, but refer to God as Infinite Intelligence. They do not accept the concept of a personal God or a personal devil. Seeing evil as the negative of good, and all of God's creations as good, Spiritualists do not believe that God created evil in the form of the devil. Evil, according to the Spiritualists, is good misunderstood and misapplied by man. Spiritualists believe in religious truths recorded in the Bible and believe that Jesus was the greatest teacher and medium ever known. Spiritualists recognize the good to be found in all other religions that emphasize truth and right living, and see religion as a process of spirituality, not as a theology, dogma, or creed.[4] (For a complete list of the Spiritualists' Declaration of Principles, see page 114).

Cassadaga regularly hosts church services on Sundays and Wednesday nights, and practices Spiritual Healing on the same days. The village also sponsors an ongoing series of workshops, seminars, and classes dealing with various aspects of Spiritualism. The Southern Cassadaga Spiritualist Camp Meeting Association offers educational programs designed to certify students as healers, mediums, and ordained ministers. The certification pro-

The Colby Memorial Temple was Cassadaga's first building. The temple was first constructed in 1895, but was torn down in 1923 to build the auditorium shown here. The Colby Memorial Temple seats 700 people and is the center of community life in Cassadaga.

cess for mediums and healers can take four to six years to complete, and to become a minister takes an additional two to four years.

Reverend Jim Watson has been living and practicing Spiritualism in Cassadaga since 1987. He says that, despite public misconceptions about Spiritualism, it is an inclusive and positive organized religion: "A Spiritualist service is basically the same as an orthodox service except for a few things. One is that one of the basic tenets of our religion is that we believe in the Continuity of Life, so during every service that we have, there is always a demonstration of the Continuity of Life, or what we call giving messages. We also do what we call hands-on healing, which is something that you see other religions do, but we take it to a little bit more extreme. The misconceptions about Spiritualism range from the sublime to the ridiculous. I guess the major thing is that people believe that there is any connection to magic, which is not true—there's no connection whatsoever with any type of magic. Then there's also the connection with the devil, that is hard to even imagine since we don't believe in a personal devil, and actually don't believe in a personal God. I want to explain that because that was hard for me, when I first came here, what we call Impersonal God. I always didn't like that term 'impersonal,' but the more I understood it, the more I thought that it was a very good thing, because it meant a God who was concerned with everybody. We have Natural Law, which makes everybody equal. You have the same opportunity in life as everybody else."[5]

While Cassadaga's church services, workshops, and seminars are well attended, the majority of people who visit the village have no connection to Spiritualism as a religion. The residents of Cassadaga, as certified mediums, give private readings to thousands of people every year. A telephone is available in the bookstore and information center at the entrance to Cassadaga, on which visitors can call a medium and schedule a reading.

Photographer Gary Monroe, a professor at Daytona Beach Community College, organized a group of scholars to put together the Cassadaga Project. The group is documenting the religion, history, folklife, and material culture of Cassadaga. Monroe was surprised to discover the diversity of people who come to Cassadaga for personal readings from a medium: "More and more people are attracted here, and more and more people are open to the possibility of mediumship. What really surprised me—who's a skeptic in his own right—for the three years that I've been coming here with this project, it seems that everybody I speak with, or most of the people I speak with outside of Cassadaga, that I would know would not have an association with Cassadaga, tends to actually have had an association with Cassadaga, or at least with psychic experience and phenomena. People in every walk of life. I suppose it addresses the New Age relevancy as well as people's desire for more total involvement with themselves and their lives, to better understand the world and their life in it. I've noticed that people who have their readings done, they usually say they are incredibly accurate, and that there's no way the mediums could have known that information. It really surprised me. It's not just one or two people—I would say eighty-five percent of the people that have readings connect to them. They're not even general readings; they're rather specific and detailed, which really got me thinking about powers that we all possess, and they fine-tune."[6]

Different mediums have individual styles of giving readings. One of the residents of Cassadaga asks people to bring in a photograph of loved ones, which she does not look at. By merely touching the back of the photograph, she can tell the person getting the reading personal information about the people in the photograph. Another resident of Cassadaga does "spirit drawings" inspired by insight from the Spirit World, which she interprets for the person getting the reading. Other mediums go into trances, while some see spirits as themselves, or in symbolic forms such as a feather or a landscape. Special trumpets are used by some mediums to facilitate vocal communication with spirits.

A basic understanding of the Spiritualism that the people of Cassadaga have been practicing for more than a century provides a foundation to explore the history of the village. Cassadaga was founded in 1894 by a medium who had worked throughout the United States, successfully converting many people to Spiritualism.

In 1860, when George P. Colby was twelve years old, two significant events happened in his life. First, Colby was baptized on a frozen Minnesota lake; second, a medium gave the boy a message from his dead uncle. Colby was told that he would found a center for Spiritualists in the southern United States. Soon after these two events, Colby began demonstrating mediumship abilities of his own, which his Baptist parents strongly discouraged, to the point of using physical punishment.[7]

At the age of nineteen, Colby left the Baptist church after experiencing episodes of clairvoyance, trances, and the development of the ability to heal through touch. He began working as a medium, giving private readings and converting skeptics with séances. By speaking fluently in languages he had never learned and giving séance participants personal information that he had no way of knowing, Colby convinced many people of the power of Spiritualism.[8]

While traveling in the northwestern United States, Colby was visited by his Native American spirit guide, named Seneca. The guide repeated the message received years earlier from Colby's uncle, that he was going to establish a Spiritualist community in the south, and added that Colby must first go to Wisconsin. Following the instructions, Colby met Spiritualist T. D. Giddings, who accompanied him to Florida. The train stopped in Jacksonville, but the men continued their journey into Central Florida by boat.[9]

Seneca guided Colby through unsettled woods to the land that was to become Cassadaga. For five years Colby and the Giddings family lived on the land, and in 1880 Colby filed a homestead claim for 74.44 acres. Throughout the 1880s and early 1890s Colby continued his travels across the United States, converting people to Spiritualism. In December 1894, a Spiritualist named E. W. Bond helped Colby establish Cassadaga as the winter residence of people from the Spiritualist camp in Lily Dale, New York.[10]

In January 1895, Colby gave a warranty deed of thirty-five acres to the Southern Cassadaga Spiritualist Camp Meeting Association, the organization that still governs life in Cassadaga. Over the years the association acquired twenty additional acres of land. In the early days of Cassadaga, Colby served as the community's spiritual leader, but he moved to New Smyrna Beach in the late 1920s. By 1933 Colby moved back to Cassadaga, where he passed on six months later.[11]

The name *Cassadaga* comes from a Seneca Indian word that means "rocks beneath the water."[12] The village took its name from a community outside the Spiritualist home of Lily Dale. The Spiritualist community was referred to as a "camp," because the early residents stayed in tents. Although most of

the buildings and homes in Cassadaga were built by the 1920s, the community is still referred to as a Spiritualist Camp.

The Colby Memorial Temple was the first building to be constructed in
Cassadaga, in 1895. The structure was remodeled in 1918, but was torn
down in 1923 to build the auditorium that is in use today. The Colby Memorial Temple seats seven hundred people and is the center of community
life in Cassadaga. Church services and classes are held in the building.

When visitors enter the main gate of Cassadaga, the first building they
see is the Cassadaga Hotel. The two-story building was constructed in 1927,
after the original three-story hotel burned down. The Cassadaga Hotel is
the only privately owned land in Cassadaga today, because in the 1930s the
association was unable to repay construction bonds it had used to build the
new hotel.

While most of the residents of Cassadaga own their homes, the Southern
Cassadaga Spiritualist Camp Association owns the property on which they
sit. Most of the homes in Cassadaga are unusual for Florida, more closely
resembling houses in New York, Maine, and Massachusetts. In addition to

The Cassadaga Hotel, constructed in 1927, is the only privately owned building in Cassadaga. In
the 1930s, the Southern Cassadaga Spiritualist Camp Meeting Association lost ownership of the
building when it was unable to repay construction bonds it had used to rebuild the hotel after
a fire. While most of the residents of Cassadaga own their homes, the association owns the
property on which they sit.

The Summerland House, built in 1926, is currently the business offices of the Southern Cassadaga Spiritualist Camp Meeting Association. Cassadaga is recognized as the oldest active religious community in the southeastern United States and is designated an historic district on the National Register of Historic Places.

the Colby Memorial Temple, the association owns the Caesar Forman Healing Center, an octagonal building created by enclosing a gazebo. The association also owns the Summerland House, the Andrew Jackson Davis Building, and two apartment buildings.

Built in 1926, the Summerland House was the home of the fifth president of the National Spiritualist Association for twenty years. Today the house is used as the business offices of the Southern Cassadaga Spiritualist Camp Meeting Association. Like the other buildings in Cassadaga, the Summerland House looks like it was designed to be built in the northeastern United States.[13]

The Andrew Jackson Davis Building houses the Cassadaga Bookstore and Information Center and was built in 1905. The building was named for the man who predicted the rise of modern Spiritualism. Sitting directly across from the Cassadaga Hotel at the entrance to the village, the Andrew Jackson Davis Building was the site of concerts, dances, and an annual masquerade ball in the early days of the community.

Harmony Hall is an eight-unit apartment building constructed in 1896. In the early 1980s the building was renovated to give each apartment its own bathroom. Brigham Hall was built as a private home in 1897, but was purchased by the association in 1913 to be used as an apartment building. The house was originally divided into eighteen single rooms, but today the home is rented as four separate apartments.

The historical significance of Cassadaga is obvious, since it is the oldest active religious community in the southeastern United States. Regardless of their religious persuasion or personal philosophy, Central Floridians should acknowledge the unique cultural contribution that Cassadaga gives to the area.

The following is the Declaration of Principles adopted by the Spiritualists of America:

1. We believe in Infinite Intelligence.
2. We believe that the phenomena of nature, both physical and spiritual, are the expression of Infinite Intelligence.
3. We affirm that a correct understanding of such expression and living in accordance therewith constitute true religion.
4. We affirm that the existence and personal identity of the individual continue after the change called death.
5. We affirm that communication with the so-called dead is a fact, scientifically proven by the phenomena of Spiritualism.
6. We believe that the highest morality is contained in the Golden Rule: "Whatsoever ye would that others should do unto you, do ye also unto them."
7. We affirm the moral responsibility of the individual, and that he makes his own happiness or unhappiness as he obeys or disobeys Nature's physical and spiritual laws.
8. We affirm that the doorway to reformation is never closed against any human soul, here or hereafter.
9. We affirm that the Precepts of Prophecy and Healing contained in the Bible are Divine attributes proven through Mediumship.[14]

❀ Barberville

Pioneer Settlement for the Creative Arts

Despite the urban sprawl of Central Florida, isolated small towns still exist in the region. Communities like Deltona, Geneva, and Zellwood retain a sense of geographic independence, surrounded by woods, farms, and undeveloped land. Barberville, a rural small town in west Volusia County, is actively preserving the history of Central Florida. At the Pioneer Settlement for the Creative Arts, historic buildings are physically preserved, and year-round demonstrations of folk crafts and the pioneer lifestyle culminate in the annual Fall Jamboree.

Barberville was named for James D. Barber in 1882, but the Barber family lived in the area as early as the 1830s. During the Civil War, cattleman Moses Barber supplied meat to the Confederate Army. After the war Barber refused to pay taxes. This caused a feud with fellow cattleman David Mizell, who was also the sheriff and tax collector. To compensate for the uncollected taxes, Mizell would periodically take some of Barber's cattle. After Barber threatened to kill Mizell, the sheriff was murdered. Deputy Sheriff David Mizell, Jr., apprehended the Barber "gang" and shot them as they tried to escape.[1]

In 1882, James D. Barber, a descendant of Moses Barber, opened the first store in Barberville with D. F. Morrison. For two years the store was called Barber and Morrison's General Merchandise. In 1884, Barber bought his partner out and renamed the store J. D. Barber's General Merchandise. Barber was also instrumental in bringing the railroad to Barberville and served as the first depot agent.[2]

Other people gradually began establishing homes and farms in Barberville during the mid and late 1800s. The area was a convenient intersection linking Pierson and Seville to the north, DeLeon Springs and DeLand to the south, Ormond Beach and Daytona Beach to the east, and Astor and Ocala to the west.

Volusia County historian Harold D. Cardwell, Sr., explains that Barberville has not changed much in more than a century: "First it was a crossroads, meaning a road going north and south and east and west. The east-and-west road came from the coast over to the river, where steamboat traffic was the main mode of transportation before the Civil War and some time after the Civil War until the railroad came through. The railroad also came through Barberville, but it's still rural and agricultural. It started out from a Naval Stores operation, where they gathered gum from pine trees. They chipped the bark off, and the gum ran into clay cups. They gathered the gum and then it went to a turpentine still. Turpentine and rosin were the two products of the Naval Store. Then a sawmill and logging industry and citrus came. Today they have ferneries, and people in the area have homes on farms, with a cattle industry in and near Barberville. It's just an agricultural community and a crossroads."[3]

The focal point of the Barberville community is now the Pioneer Settlement for the Creative Arts, located near the intersection of Highway 17 and State Road 40. The ten-acre site is the home of a collection of historic buildings situated to resemble a pioneer settlement. The settlement is a not-for-profit corporation managed by the Volusia County School Board. More than twenty-five thousand school children are taken to the settlement every year to see the historic structures and to witness demonstrations of folk crafts such as weaving, cotton-spinning, and candle-dipping. An additional thirty-five thousand people visit the settlement yearly.[4]

The centerpiece of the Pioneer Settlement for the Creative Arts is the Barberville School, built in 1919. The school is the only building in the settlement that is in its original location. Grades 1 through 12 attended the Barberville School until 1940, when the last senior class of four students graduated. Grades 1 through 6 then attended the school until 1966, when the Volusia County School Board declared the building unsuitable as an educational facility.[5]

The Barberville School was put up for sale, but no buyer was found. The building was used as a storage facility and then abandoned. Marilyn Breeze, a Volusia County teacher and director of the Pioneer Settlement for the Creative Arts, explains how the area around the Barberville School was developed into a site for historic preservation: "In 1976 a group of art teachers got together and decided they'd have an arts settlement. They had visions of having an art colony where people could come here and enrich themselves and grow in their arts, and at the same time preserve the history and do the folk arts. Our focus has changed somewhat since those early days. We're probably more on the social studies and history end of the spectrum at this point, preserving our local past. We're collecting buildings that are representative of a village."[6]

While a few of the buildings in the Pioneer Settlement are reproduc-

The Barberville School, built in 1919, is the centerpiece of the Pioneer Settlement for the Creative Arts. In 1966, the Volusia County School Board declared the building unsuitable as an educational facility. The Barberville School is the only building now in the Pioneer Settlement for the Creative Arts that was located there originally.

tions, most are historic structures that were saved from demolition by being relocated.

At the entrance to the settlement is the Astor Bridge House. The building, constructed in the 1920s, served as the home of the bridge tender in Astor, a small town located near where State Road 40 crosses the St. Johns River, west of Barberville. The structure is one of the few existing bridge tender's homes in Florida and was moved to Barberville in 1983.

Although the turpentine industry was active in Barberville, the Tomoka Turpentine Still in the Pioneer Settlement was originally located near Daytona. Constructed in the 1920s, the still was in operation for about twenty years and was moved to its present location in 1988.

The Commissary Store is one of the oldest buildings in the settlement. Constructed in 1884, the store served the Central Florida community of Bakersburg. The store was relocated to Barberville in 1984 and is stocked as it would have been in the late 1800s.

The Tomoka Turpentine Still, built in the 1920s, has been relocated to Barberville. More than twenty-five thousand schoolchildren are taken to the Pioneer Settlement for the Creative Arts every year to see the historic structures and witness folk crafts such as weaving, cotton spinning, and candle dipping.

The Huntington Post Office, built in 1885, is now located in Barberville. The building was brought to the Pioneer Settlement for the Creative Arts in 1996 and outfitted with period equipment. The post office was originally located near Crescent City.

Originally located near Crescent City, the Huntington Post Office was constructed in 1885. Refurbished to its former condition and outfitted with period equipment, the post office was brought to the Pioneer Settlement in 1996.

The community of Pierson is a neighbor of Barberville. The Pierson Railroad Depot was constructed in the 1880s and remained active for almost a century. The depot was relocated to Barberville in 1984. The caboose that sits in front of the depot was built in 1960.

In 1993, the DeLand District of the United Methodist Church donated an historic church to the Pioneer Settlement for the Creative Arts. The Midway United Methodist Church was moved to the settlement in 1994 and was restored the following year. Built in 1890, the church was used for worship services until 1964.[7]

The Pottery Shed at the settlement was a private workshop constructed in the 1920s. Originally located in DeLeon Springs, the structure was moved to its current site in 1989.

The Midway United Methodist Church, built in 1890, was in use until 1964. During the annual Fall Jamboree at the Pioneer Settlement for the Creative Arts, the church is used for musical performances and lectures.

The Lewis Log Cabin is the only non-Florida building in the Pioneer Settlement. The home was built in south Georgia in 1870. The descendants of Jim Lewis, the builder of the cabin, purchased the home in 1991 and had it moved to Barberville the following year.

To augment the collection of historic buildings in the Pioneer Settlement, several reproductions of period structures have been assembled. The Settlement Firehouse was built in 1986 to house two antique fire engines and to serve as a firehouse museum. The late-1800s-style Wood Shop was constructed in 1993. The Blacksmith Shop, built in 1988, resembles an early-twentieth-century shop and is outfitted with antique equipment. The replica of a turn-of-the-century barn was constructed in 1986.

The Pioneer Settlement for the Creative Arts continues to collect historic buildings, saving them from destruction. Marilyn Breeze says that as recently as early 1997, renovations continued on an early-twentieth-century house brought to Barberville: "We tore down a building in New Smyrna, when the city was having an urban renewal type of thing. They were taking down some old vacant houses that they were worried about becoming crack houses. We've salvaged one of them. Some of them went to John Singleton's *Rosewood* film project, and we got this one. We're going to use it as a Turpentine Quarters House, a type of structure that the workers at a turpentine still back in the early 1900s would have lived in. One of our staff members is very eager to outfit this."[8]

All of the buildings in the Pioneer Settlement are outfitted with antique tools, equipment, and other artifacts appropriate to the function of the structure. The barn yard is stocked with live sheep, geese, peacocks, and other animals. Staff members and volunteers give demonstrations of how early pioneers in Central Florida lived and worked. An annual festival at the settlement attracts hundreds of people interested in demonstrating and displaying folk arts and crafts.

The annual Fall Jamboree, initiated in 1977, is held the first full weekend in November. Skilled folk artists from throughout the state show visitors how local settlers created their own quilts, rugs, furniture, musical instruments, clothing, baskets, tools, and other necessities of daily life. Blacksmithing and farming techniques are demonstrated, and nonstop entertainment is provided by musicians and storytellers. Homemade food such as barbecued chicken, corn on the cob, boiled peanuts, and desserts are available.

Although a Native American camp is not a permanent component of the Pioneer Settlement for the Creative Arts, one is erected for the Fall Jamboree. Timucuan and Seminole living quarters are built, and their cooking and sewing methods are described. Costumed storytellers explain Native American beliefs and traditions. Visitors can try grinding corn with stones and play with handcrafted toys.

The inhabitants of Barberville look forward to the Fall Jamboree and support the year-round activities of the Pioneer Settlement. Lifelong Barberville resident John Jerico was born in 1922 on the eighty-acre sheep farm he now operates. Jerico is the son of Austrian-born Louis Jerico and Ohio native Henrietta Zelda. A classically trained violinist, Louis Jerico worked as a carpenter, a prison guard, and a road construction worker after moving to Central Florida in 1921. Henrietta Zelda was the postmistress of nearby Emporia from 1926 to 1953.[9]

John Jerico and his wife, Fran, are volunteer demonstrators at the settle-ment. He emphasizes the continuity of life in Barberville: "Barberville hasn't changed a whole lot in seventy-five years. It stays about the same. About the same number of residents now as there was. They put the popu-lation at about three thousand—that means scattered all over the woods too. I talk to schoolchildren on field trips at the settlement. I think it's a good thing for them to come by and understand how we did live back seventy-five or eighty years ago in this area. I tell 'em all about the farm. I show 'em what we did, what we grow down there. We have our sheep, and we have chickens and things down there, and a duck. We have a mule and a donkey out there. I have to give them a talk on that and how to feed 'em. My wife mostly spins on the spinning wheel. She spins wool and cotton. We do raise our own sheep at the settlement. We have 'em sheared once a year, and we do raise cotton down there too."[10] Volunteers at the Pioneer Settlement also demonstrate indigo dying, cane grinding, log milling, wood carving, and other folk crafts.

While the annual Fall Jamboree is the primary fund-raising event for the Pioneer Settlement, a variety of other festivals and concerts are held there throughout the year. Various events focusing on multicultural arts and crafts are presented, and ethnic concerts are performed. A tool exhibition is held at the settlement, and the Florida Artist Blacksmith Association has an an-nual event there. Harold D. Cardwell, Sr., believes that the Pioneer Settle-ment is a valuable resource for Central Floridians: "For education, it's a way to step back into yesterday and to see all of the tools and appliances that our forefathers used, and how buildings were constructed. They teach the vari-ous craft skills that we don't want to lose. I believe as time goes on, the settlement will grow. It will offer even more for helping with the education of schoolchildren, high school students, and even adults to go over for fes-tivals and craft shows and tool shows and so forth."[11]

The activities at the Pioneer Settlement for the Creative Arts are excellent examples of how the history of Central Florida can help to create a sense of community in the present. By going to Barberville and learning about local history, residents can feel a new connection to the region. Visitors to the area can also benefit by enjoying an educational cultural experience in Barberville.

❊ Daytona Beach

Spring Break, Bike Week, Auto Racing . . . and the London Symphony Orchestra

Orlando is not the only Central Florida city that suffers from a public misconception of its cultural identity. The greater Orlando area has much more to offer residents and visitors than a trip to Disney World, Sea World, or Universal Studios. Likewise, there is much more to Daytona Beach than just "fun in the sun."

When most people think of Daytona Beach, the first thing that comes to mind is Spring Break. Every year thousands of teenagers and young adults from across the country descend on Daytona Beach for a carnal celebration of drinking to excess, sex, sunbathing, and free concerts at the 1930s coquina bandshell.

Just before Spring Break begins for the year, the rumble of Harley-Davidsons and other motorcycles can be heard throughout Daytona as Bike Week, another well-known tradition, gets under way in the first week of March. Bike Week brings legions of full-time bikers to Daytona, as well as a large group of businessmen, teachers, professionals, and other people who don their leather clothing once a year to participate in the revelry.

Daytona is also a mecca for auto-racing fans. Since the early twentieth century, auto racing has been prevalent there, when racing pioneers like Alexander Winston and Ransom Olds set speed records approaching sixty miles an hour on the firm sands of Daytona Beach. Today the Daytona International Speedway is the home of the Daytona 500 and other important auto races.[1]

Fossil remains discovered in Daytona indicate that primitive people lived in the area from at least 5000 B.C. In more recent centuries the area that is now Daytona was inhabited by Native American tribes including the Timucua, Miccosukee, and Seminoles.[2] The series of Seminole Indian Wars that began in 1817 eventually forced Native Americans out of the region.

The city of Daytona was incorporated in 1876. The town was named in honor of Mathias Day, an entrepreneur from Ohio who moved to Central Florida in 1871 to develop land along the Halifax River.[3] Although Day is Daytona's namesake, a wealthy pioneer named Charles Grover Burgoyne contributed more to the growth of the city.

Charles Grover Burgoyne fought in the Civil War, joining the Union Army at age fourteen. After the war, Burgoyne made a fortune in the printing business, with important clients like American Express, the Western Union Telegraph Company, and the Union Pacific Railway. Burgoyne moved to Daytona in 1894 and through his investments was largely responsible for transforming the city into a thriving residential community and a popular tourist destination.[4]

After serving as Daytona's mayor from 1897 to 1898, Burgoyne contrib-

The Daytona International Speedway continues the city's long tradition of auto racing, with events like the Daytona 500. In the early twentieth century auto races were held on the beach at Daytona, where racing pioneers such as Alexander Winston and Ransom Olds set speed records.

uted large amounts of money to the Halifax River Yacht Club.[5] Burgoyne
regularly paid for public concerts at a bandstand he had built downtown.
A ten-foot-wide concrete promenade lined with streetlights was named
the Esplanade Burgoyne in honor of its benefactor. In 1916, Burgoyne built
and operated the Burgoyne Casino in downtown Daytona, which burned
down in 1937. Burgoyne died on March 31, 1916, but the tradition of cultural events that he established continues in Daytona today.[6]

In addition to Daytona's many transient and seasonal residents, local
families enjoy cultural offerings like the Friends of the Bandshell concerts,
the Seaside Music Theater, and the Southeast Museum of Photography year-
round. Daytona is also the permanent home of several well-respected educational institutions such as Embry-Riddle Aeronautical University, the tra-
ditionally African American Bethune-Cookman College, and Daytona Beach
Community College.

The Museum of Arts and Sciences in Daytona presents touring exhibitions of work by important artists and craftsmen and has an eclectic permanent collection of art, crafts, furniture, and antique personal items. Gary
Libby, director of the Museum of Arts and Sciences, explains that much of

The Tarragona Arch, built in the mid-1920s, was originally half of a pair of Spanish-style arches.
The other arch was destroyed during the construction of Daytona Beach Community College,
which is across the street from the surviving arch. DBCC is the home of the Southeast Museum
of Photography and the Seaside Music Theater.

the institution's focus is on preserving our cultural heritage: "I think that 'Cuba: A History in Art' is an excellent example of an important collection, brought here by the Batistas after the Cuban Revolution, that now functions as a national collection in exile for over a million and a half Cuban Floridians. The 'Arts in America' collection and the Bouchelle Center for the International Decorative Arts are collections put together by significant Floridians, collections that will become a base for understanding aesthetics, and understanding quality in design, and color and light for generations of students who come here to see original objects. I think this and other museums, especially through their visual-arts collections, are in the forefront of writing the history of the next century. Many of the objects in the permanent collections of Florida museums are doing that. They're a new baseline for understanding of a lot of the highest aspirations in Western culture."[7]

Local cultural contributions are recognized with a festival presented in Daytona's historic district. Since 1993, an annual event called Old Daytona Days has been held the weekend before Thanksgiving. Old Daytona Days celebrates the history of the area through Civil War battle reenactments and a tour of historic homes and sites.

Vinton Fisher, chairman of the Old Daytona Civic Association, organizes Old Daytona Days. He describes some of the historical figures remembered in the event: "The people that we recognize include folks like Colonel Williams, who founded the first plantation in this area, called the Orange Grove Plantation. It goes back to 1790. His heirs eventually sold the land to Mathias Day in 1870, leading to the founding of Daytona. We recognize the impact of the Civil War, which goes back to 1866, when Freemanville was founded by Dr. and Mrs. Hawkes, who were abolitionists, and African American Union soldiers who were veterans. The founding of Freemanville preceded the founding of Daytona.

"We also recognize figures like Mr. Rhodes, Mr. Gamble, Mr. White, Mr. Rockefeller, and Mr. Olds, who were the persons who brought speed to Daytona, because Rockefeller, in oil, brought his friend Ford down, Olds, and then Winston, the inventor of the V-8 engine. Both Rhodes and White were supporters of very important African American leader Mary McLeod Bethune. There was a direct linkage between the wealthy wintering people in old Daytona, and Mrs. Bethune. Jackie Robinson Stadium is right in the heart of our neighborhood. On St. Patrick's Day, March the seventeenth, 1946, Jackie Robinson broke into baseball, playing for the Montreal Royals, a farm team of the Brooklyn Dodgers. Robinson broke baseball's color line in Daytona, when he wasn't allowed to play in other area towns. We also recognize theologian Dr. Howard Thurman, the mentor of Dr. Martin Luther King."[8]

Fisher points out that much of Daytona's history, from the establishment of Freemanville to the Civil Rights movement of the 1960s, centers around African Americans. Many of the descendants of Freemanville's original inhabitants still reside in Daytona, and the legacy of Mary McLeod Bethune lives on at Bethune-Cookman College.

Mary McLeod Bethune rose to international recognition despite being the daughter of former slaves. Bethune was the fifteenth of seventeen children and the first in her family to be born free. The all-girl school that Bethune established in Daytona in 1904 merged with Jacksonville's Cookman Institute for Boys in 1923, to form Bethune-Cookman College.[9]

The house where Bethune lived and died is on the college campus that bears her name. The two-story frame house, built in 1914, is now the home of the Mary McLeod Bethune Foundation. Bethune and former First Lady Eleanor Roosevelt established the foundation, which preserves African American history through the exhibition of photographs and artifacts.

The birthplace of Howard Thurman, built around 1888, is also in Daytona.[10] In 1953 *Life* magazine named Thurman "one of the 12 greatest preachers of the twentieth century."[11] Thurman preached racial equality through nonviolent change before Martin Luther King, Jr., did, and he was this country's primary contact with Mahatma Gandhi for many years. The Thurman home, at 614 Whitehall Street in Daytona, was renovated in 1984.[12]

Another example of the cultural heritage of Central Florida that can be enjoyed in Daytona Beach is the Florida International Festival. For more than two weeks every other year, the Florida International Festival brings the London Symphony Orchestra to the area for a series of classical music and pops concerts, together with a diverse group of chamber ensembles, dance companies, and unique contemporary performers.

The Florida International Festival was founded by Tippen Davidson, publisher of the Daytona Beach News Journal. The first event was held in

Mary McLeod Bethune's Home, built in 1914, now houses the Mary McLeod Bethune Foundation. The building, located on the campus of Bethune-Cookman College, contains photographs
and artifacts that preserve African American history. Mary McLeod Bethune, the daughter of
former slaves, rose to international recognition.

1966 and was repeated annually for several years. The festival was staged
more sporadically during the 1970s, but in the following decade was firmly
established as a biennial event falling on odd-numbered years.

As Davidson explains, the Florida International Festival was originally
established to fight Daytona's widespread image as a party town: "We had a
very mild version of Spring Break back in the '60s, and a wire service cor-
respondent who came by to observe coined the deathless phrase 'sex, sand,
and suds' for the rather innocent high jinks that were going on here in the
'60s. Of course the city fathers were aghast. A lot of meetings took place,
and we got together, and a lot of people had a lot of suggestions as to how
all this bad publicity could be counteracted. Fortunately we hadn't invented
the word 'image' at that point. The festival was an offshoot of one of those
meetings. There was a meeting that was called to talk about various upside
cultural and educational projects. In those days four-year colleges were
contemplating moving south to escape the winter, and we thought maybe
we could set our cap for one of those, and the music festival was just one of
the things that was discussed."[13]

Volusia County did not have an indigenous group that a significant music festival could be based around. Concerned civic leaders invited twenty-five cultural organizations from around the world to participate in a festival in Daytona. Davidson says that the only serious reply came from the London Symphony Orchestra: "We got a really stimulating answer from the London Symphony, outlining the entire festival program, setting a price, and generally just laying it on the line. The board got back together, and we were all delighted with the proposal. We raised the money in about eight days, as I recollect, one hundred and twenty thousand dollars, and we raised it in the form of guarantees, which we didn't tap the first year. From there it was smooth sailing all the way. Of course, we have to raise a lot more money now than we did then, and I can't say that it's really smooth sailing, but at least we do it."[14]

Although organizing a classical music festival is a noble effort, the civic leaders of Daytona have an ulterior motive for sponsoring the Florida International Festival. Tourism is the area's biggest industry, and the London Symphony Orchestra attracts an entirely different audience than do free rock concerts on the beach, biker bars, and auto races. In addition to the festival's enhancing Daytona's image and giving year-round residents more cultural offerings, local officials and business owners hoped it would bring a new set of tourists to the area. According to Sharron Mock, executive director of the Daytona Beach Area Convention and Visitors Bureau, the Florida International Festival has a significant economic impact on Volusia County: "Yes, I can say that it has. The Daytona Beach Area Convention and Visitors Bureau is proud to be one of the many sponsors of the festival. Our investment is returned to the community many times over through the economic impact created by our visitors, along with the positive image and cultural enrichment which the festival brings. Tourism studies indicate that a community's arts and cultural offerings are an important factor for many people when they are deciding where to spend their vacation dollars."[15]

Daytona's firm sands and warm climate are enough to entice visitors, but Mock believes that when the Florida International Festival is held, many visitors choose to come to Daytona over other beach communities: "It certainly is an added attraction. Feature stories about the festival appear in newspapers and magazines throughout the country, and in the United Kingdom. This offers the vacation visitor a new perspective on how they can spend their time in this area. Visitors come from all over Florida and the southeast to enjoy the world-famous musical talents that are showcased in the Florida International Festival."[16]

Beyond enhancing Daytona's image and bringing more tourism dollars to the area, the Florida International Festival provides audiences with many memorable performances. The festival brings important performers to the stage before they reach the height of their careers. For example, at one of the early festivals, violinist Itzak Perlman, pianist Vladimir Ashkenazy, and horn soloist Barry Tuckwell played both as soloists with the London Symphony Orchestra and in chamber concerts at churches throughout Volusia and Flagler counties, well before they were household names. More recently soprano Harolyn Blackwell appeared at the festival at around the same time she took over the Metropolitan Opera roles vacated by Kathleen Battle.

Because the London Symphony is one of the most well respected orchestras in the world, the Florida International Festival is able to attract many of the giants of classical music. Often these world-class players are willing to perform for greatly reduced fees for the opportunity to vacation on the "world's most famous beach" between concerts.

When cellist Mstislav Rostropovich performed at the 1991 Florida International Festival, he had been considered the world's greatest cello soloist for more than fifty years. Rostropovich has recorded most of the cello repertoire and has inspired many prominent composers such as Sergie Prokofiev, Benjamin Britten, Leonard Bernstein, and Dimitri Shostikovich to create works especially for him. For more than thirty years, Rostropovich had also been receiving acclaim as a conductor. At the Florida International Festival, Rostropovich has performed both as a cello soloist and conductor of the London Symphony. He describes his reaction to the area: "I first time coming in this part of Florida, first time I in Daytona, and that's fantastic place. You know I see many beautiful places in United States, but this place for me now is combined for two important things. One, of course, that's your fantastic beach, but another, that's your enthusiasm, your love for the music. That's for me a real surprise. For festival you invited the best orchestra in Great Britain—that's no doubt for me—but one of the great orchestras of course in Europe coming here—that's enormous joy, and I am so proud of United States of America."[17]

While the reputation of an orchestra ultimately rests on the combined skill of its players, much credit must also be given to the management structure that organizes rehearsal schedules, concert programs, recording sessions, and tours. Since 1985 Clive Gillanson has been the managing director of the London Symphony, and for fifteen years before that he was a cellist with the orchestra. Gillanson says his move from musician to manager was not exactly planned: "I think, like a lot of major decisions in life, this one happened by mistake. The orchestra at the time was in terrible financial problems; we had just moved into the Barbicon Center in the city, and become the first orchestra ever with a residency in London. The whole thing was an untried concept, and the orchestra entered into terrible financial problems. The manager was asked to leave, and we advertised for a new manager, and couldn't find anybody. The board at the time then decided maybe the best thing to do would be to get a player to go in, at least for three months, to give us a little bit more time to find a manager. They asked me to do it, which was basically for the not very good reason that I had run an antique business as a hobby, so they assumed that I knew all about business. I can only say that it was no preparation whatsoever for running the London Symphony Orchestra. It started off like that. I initially did it for the three months; they still couldn't find anybody, and they asked me to stay."[18]

Gillanson was unsure whether he was ready to give up being a musician to become managing director, so he proposed that he and the board give each other one year and then reevaluate the situation. Gillanson has been running the orchestra ever since.

Since the Florida International Festival was firmly established as a biennial event in the mid-1980s, two auxiliary sets of concerts have coincided with the two weeks of performances by the London Symphony Orchestra. One set of concerts features chamber music performances at churches and small auditoriums throughout Volusia, Flagler, and Seminole counties. These concerts feature well-known classical music ensembles, such as the Golub Kaplan Carr Trio and the Colorado Quartet, and soloists, such as harpist Osian Ellis and comic pianist Victor Borge.

The Coquina Bandshell on Daytona Beach, in use since the 1930s, has been the venue for everything from classical music programs to rap and rock concerts. The Friends of the Bandshell present free cultural programs every weekend from May through October. The bandshell is a block away from the Peabody Auditorium and the Ocean Center, where much of the Florida International Festival is performed.

With the hope of attracting a more varied audience to the Florida International Festival, organizers established a second set of programs, a series of nonclassical music performances to augment the event. These programs have featured performances by the José Limon Dance Company, the Pilobolus Dance Company, folk guitarist Leo Kottke, jazz pianist Marcus Roberts, the Dave Brubeck Quartet, and many others. Festival organizers hope that people who may be intimidated by the London Symphony Orchestra will be lured into attending the festival through one of the auxiliary concerts and will then give the larger programs a chance.

Perhaps the best indicator of how the London Symphony Orchestra has been integrated into the Daytona Beach community is its participation in the Southern Bell Youth Ensemble. During each Florida International Festival approximately twenty high school students studying instrumental music are selected by audition to study with members of the London Symphony Orchestra in intensive workshops. The experience culminates with the members of the youth ensemble performing with the orchestra in a special Young People's Concert for area children.

Richard McNichol founded the Apollo Trust, an organization in Great Britain dedicated to instructing children in the performance of classical music, and he was selected to lead the Southern Bell Youth Ensemble at the 1995 Florida International Festival. He discusses music education for children: "We have a rather strange situation at home in that, by law, every child between the age of five and fourteen must be taught to compose, and must be taught to perform. That's every single child in school. You can imagine that teachers have suddenly found themselves with quite a problem. The aim of all our programs now that we do with the orchestra is to involve children in live music-making. This of course is part of it. Everybody invents, everybody performs, and music becomes a practical subject, not a theoretical one. We want to help them to play at their absolute top standard. The other thing we can do, because Daytona is now awash with professional musicians from the London Symphony Orchestra, is to involve them in the music we make."[19]

Other educational opportunities offered by the Florida International Festival include the availability of in-service-hour verification for Florida music teachers and the option of earning credit toward graduate degree programs for those who participate in specially designed festival events.

The London Symphony Orchestra has named Daytona Beach its official summer home. Cynics might argue that the orchestra is merely playing another series of performances in a long line of concerts every other year and that their residency in Daytona does not mean that they are really a part of the community. Festival organizers, the members of the orchestra, and people in the Daytona community would strongly disagree. Unlike on other concert tours, the members of the London Symphony Orchestra bring their families along when making their biennial trek to Central Florida. Two marriages have occurred between members of the orchestra and residents of Daytona. Orchestra Chairman John Lawley readily acknowledges that Daytona is truly a home away from home for the orchestra musicians and that they do feel strong ties to the community: "I would absolutely guarantee that they do. Particularly some of the older ones like myself. I'm now on my seventh visit. Obviously we've got a lot of close friends here now. There is a community feeling that we don't get anywhere else we go. Normally you just go to a big city in the world, you do a concert, and you go out. The great thing here is that we're here for up to two weeks, and you do feel a part of the community. It's a small community, a very intensely aware community, and they're very involved with us. It's a reciprocal thing, you get it back."[20]

Since founding the Florida International Festival in 1966, director Tippen Davidson has enjoyed watching the close bonds between the London Symphony Orchestra and the Daytona Beach community grow: "The living evidence is when you go to the airport to see the LSO get off the plane, the big grins on their faces as they get off, the hugs and the handshaking. It's quite evident that they're happy to be here."[21] Daytona always gives the London Symphony Orchestra a royal welcome when they arrive, complete with a parade through the center of town.

Although the London Symphony Orchestra is obviously not an indigenous Central Florida group, the Florida International Festival has become an important community-spirited cultural celebration for the area. Tippen Davidson is pleased with how the festival has permeated the heart of Daytona: "This festival is an outstanding example of starting at the top. We began this festival with one of the great orchestras of the world, with the world's great conductors, with the finest soloists that could be had anywhere. This was tops. The New York Times wrote about us the first year, 'no finer concerts are to be heard anywhere in the world'. That's exactly what we wanted. We couldn't help, if we found any kind of financial support, we couldn't help but go anywhere but up."[22]

Daytona Beach will probably always be regarded by outsiders as a popular Spring Break destination for college students, a haven for motorcycle enthusiasts, and a center for auto racing. These annual events are undeniably a significant part of Central Florida culture. However, Daytona is also rich in African American history, and, for two weeks in late July and early August every other year, the city becomes the home of one of the best celebrations of music and the arts in the world.

❊ New Smyrna Beach

The Artistic Foresight of Doris Leeper

New Smyrna Beach is located south of Daytona. While tourists gravitate to "the world's most famous beach," Central Floridians often prefer the less-congested ambience of New Smyrna Beach. The quiet, artistic community is one of the first to be established in Florida.

The British took control of Florida from Spain in 1762. At that time Central Florida was virtually uninhabited. A Scotsman named Andrew Turnbull arranged to bring Greek and Minorcan settlers to New Smyrna Beach in 1767. Turnbull envisioned a colony that would grow cotton and other crops to trade with Great Britain.[1] The journey from Greece to America was plagued by rough weather and sickness, and 148 of the 1,403 people that Turnbull was bringing to Central Florida died before the ships arrived.[2]

Turnbull was a harsh administrator of justice, and many colonists died under his rule. Disease, starvation, and harsh working conditions killed more of New Smyrna's first European settlers.[3] By 1777, many of the remaining colonists revolted and migrated to St. Augustine.[4] When the British returned control of Florida to Spain in 1783, few of the Greeks, Minorcans, Italians, and Corsicans living in New Smyrna chose to stay there.[5]

New settlers gradually repopulated New Smyrna in the early 1800s.[6] The oldest architectural structure in Central Florida is in New Smyrna Beach. The partially destroyed sugar mill is one of sixteen such buildings constructed between St. Augustine and New Smyrna Beach after the United States took control of Florida in 1821. The sugar mill, destroyed during the Second Seminole Indian War in 1835, is protected as the New Smyrna Sugar Mill Ruins Historic Park.[7] Visitors can see the crumbling coquina walls of the sugar mill, cast-iron vats used to cook the sugar cane, and an old sugar press used to make syrup. A group of modern buildings near the sugar mill is the site of important artistic collaborations.

Tucked away on sixty-seven acres of pine and palmetto forest just outside of New Smyrna Beach is the Atlantic Center for the Arts. Since the early 1980s the Atlantic Center for the Arts has brought together diverse groups of composers, writers, playwrights, choreographers, and visual artists to work among the trees overlooking the tidal estuary Turnbull Bay. When internationally known painter and sculptor Doris Leeper founded the Atlantic Center, she was concerned that the facility's buildings would not disrupt the natural setting of the site. Even after a massive expansion of the facility,

The New Smyrna Sugar Mill, built in 1821, is the oldest architectural structure in Central Florida. The mill was partially destroyed in 1835, during the Second Seminole Indian War. Visitors to the New Smyrna Sugar Mill Ruins Historic Park can see the crumbling coquina walls of the mill, cast-iron vats used to cook sugar cane, and an old sugar press used to make syrup.

the center sits on just ten acres of the property overlooking the bay. Leeper explains the vision she had: "The model for the Atlantic Center in spirit was my place down at Canaveral National Seashore. We said if we could arrange to get some waterfront somewhere, and keep that natural environment, and do everything we could not to disturb the environment, the wonderful sense that I had at my place there could be transferred to the Center, and in fact that's what happened."[8]

Leeper moved to Eldora, Florida, on the Indian River Lagoon, in 1961 and was instrumental in establishing the area as the Canaveral National Seashore, again helping to preserve Florida's natural environment for future generations. After leaving her hometown of Charlotte, North Carolina, Leeper graduated from Duke University with a degree in art history before moving to Florida. Her paintings and large site-specific sculptures have been displayed around the world, including shows at the National Museum of Art in Washington, D.C., the Ringling Museum of Art in Florida, Tennessee's Hunter Museum, and Wadsworth Athenaeum in Hartford, Connecticut.

As an active artist, Leeper had an opportunity to participate in various traditional artist residencies. Although the traditional artist residency allows artists within one discipline to be isolated and produce innovative work, Leeper was interested in exploring what could be accomplished with interdisciplinary artist residencies: "I was in North Carolina, doing a residency for the Rockefeller Foundation, a sculpture residency, and I noticed that around the city some wonderful things were going on in dance, in theater, in visual arts, and so forth, but generally speaking they weren't collaborating certainly, and they hardly knew of each other's existence. It seemed to me that if all of those things could happen in one place, everybody's creative energy could be shared."[9]

A distinguished list of master artists has worked and collaborated at the Atlantic Center for the Arts. They include composer Lukas Foss, author James Dickey, sculptor Duane Hanson, playwright and director Edward Albee, United States poet laureate Howard Nemerov, composer Milton Babbitt, choreographer Trisha Brown, and photographer William Wegman. The Atlantic Center's artist residencies often result in completed collaborative projects. Executive Director Suzanne Fetcher describes some of the projects worked on at the Atlantic Center: "Pieces that have been produced here or have been developed while the master artists are in residence include *Historias,* which is a piece collaborated on by Pepon Osorio, who is a visual artist, Merion Soto, who is a choreographer, and Carl Royce, who is a composer. From here they premiered it at the Jacob's Pillow Dance Festival, and from there went to Lincoln Center. We've had other similar projects developed here. Kei Takei, who is a Japanese-born choreographer living in the United States, was here in residence with Yukio Tsuji, who is a composer, and Ichi Ikeda, who is a visual artist who also designs sets for theater and dance pieces, and David Moss who is a vocalist. They were here working on a piece called *Twenty-Four Hours of Light,* and they took it from here to the Walker Art Center in Minneapolis, where it was premiered also."[10]

While many interesting collaborative performance-art projects have come out of the Atlantic Center artist residencies, many artists choose to take advantage of the serene natural surroundings of the center to contemplate individual projects. For example, composer John Corigliano wrote portions of his opera *The Ghost of Versailles* at the Atlantic Center preceding its premiere at the New York City Opera, and Russian composer Rodion Shchedrin worked on his piano concerto there prior to its National Symphony Orchestra premiere under the direction of Mstislav Rostropovich. Although important work is done at the Atlantic Center, the resident artists are under no obligation or mandate to create art while they are in residence.

In addition to having the opportunity to collaborate with artists from other disciplines or to work on individual projects while at the Atlantic Center, the master artists work with selected associate artists from their own disciplines while in residence. Associate artists are mid-career artists who have already established themselves and received some recognition for their artistic integrity and vision. While at the Atlantic Center, the master artists and their associate artists meet for three hours a day as a group, discussing issues and concerns, and then spend the rest of the day pursuing their own individual projects. The combination of intense informative discussions and time to reflect on those discussions informs and influences each artist's work.

After participating in a residency, master artists often continue their affiliation with the Atlantic Center. Edward Albee, one of the first master artists in residence, still supports the Atlantic Center's efforts. The author of

The Atlantic Center for the Arts, built in the early 1980s, was designed to blend in with the surrounding pine and palmetto forest. Founder Doris Leeper wanted to create a cultural center that would host interdisciplinary artist residencies. A diverse group of composers, playwrights, choreographers, and visual artists have worked and taught at the Atlantic Center for the Arts.

the plays *Who's Afraid of Virginia Woolf?*, *Seascape*, *The Sandbox*, and *Three Tall Women*, Albee serves on the National Advisory Council of the Atlantic Center for the Arts. He recounts: "I was one of the first creative artists to work here back in 1982, with Reynolds Price, the novelist, and Mia Westerlund, the sculptor. We were all good friends, we all came down together. The ability for people to come and work together in a nice location like this for three weeks, with concentration, seemed like a very good thing. I've watched it from the very first days develop from just a couple of buildings into this enormous complex. It seems to have established itself, finally, as an important and useful arts center. Those of us who are on the National Advisory Council—we've all been master artists here at one time or another—are trying to keep the place honest. It isn't that difficult. I like the cross-pollination that comes with people in different disciplines sometimes working together, or having students that get to intermingle."[11]

The incredible range of artistic expression explored at the Atlantic Center is evident in the work of the individual artists who have been in residence there. Poet Sonia Sanchez has published more than a dozen books of poetry, including *Homecoming, Homegirls and Handgrenades,* and *Under a Soprano Sky.* Sanchez is also a contributing editor to *Black Scholar* and the *Journal of African Studies.*

In the late 1960s Sanchez taught in the country's first black studies program at San Francisco State College, and in the early 1970s she taught black culture and literature classes at the University of Pittsburgh and Rutgers University. Sanchez's latest work is a collection of poetry called *Wounded in the House of a Friend.* In the book Sanchez explores personal and societal wounds. She explains: "'Wounded in the house of a friend' comes from the Bible, Zechariah 13, verse 6, and it talks about the wounds we have in our hands. We are experiencing wounds in this country and in the world. Some of them are personal wounds from personal relationships between men and women; some of the wounds are wounds we have with the whole idea of crack, that is wiping out a certain segment of our people in our country, and many of the wounds are happening worldwide—on the continent of Africa, Rwanda, India, Latin America.

"What I'm saying is that at some point we must look at these wounds and begin the real process of healing these wounds. We are trying to move to the twenty-first century, and we don't need this baggage that started perhaps at the turn of the twentieth century. We need to look at the world and say simply, 'We can support you, earth, we can guarantee that you will survive.' At the same time we've got to guarantee the earth that we will not pollute it, we will not destroy it in any way. We pollute the waters, the skies, we cut down rain forests. We've got to say finally, 'We can't survive if we do this.' We certainly can't survive as human beings if we don't respect each other and open up to the different cultures that exist on this earth."[12]

While she was a master artist in residence at the Atlantic Center for the Arts, Sanchez worked with six selected associate artists whom she chose based on work that they submitted. Each day of the six-week residency, Sanchez and her associates read and critiqued each other's poetry: "When you open up to all of these different voices, you get a sense of the world, and what can be. That's the joy of listening to the many voices here. African Americans, Native Americans, Asian writers, people who are writing about what it means to be human on this planet, coming from their own specific culture. It is something to read it and to look at, and to learn something new and anew each time."[13]

Contemporary classical composer Chinary Ung has also been an artist in residence at the Atlantic Center for the Arts. Ung was born in Cambodia in 1942 and came to America in 1964 to further his musical studies. Ung received his doctor of musical arts degree from Columbia University and has since received many awards, grants, and commissions for his work. Unlike many contemporary classical composers, Ung has enjoyed having his pieces recorded and performed often. Listeners to Ung's music notice that while he likes to experiment with sound, he also has much respect for musical tradition. Although Ung says he does not consciously blend the music of his native Cambodia with western classical music, listeners hear a synthesis of eastern and western traditions in Ung's work: "Let's say blue color represents western tradition and yellow color represents eastern tradition. When you mix the two, obviously it turns out to be green. How much greener depends on the individual. As to my view, elements that are drawn from tradition, not all of them are good, so you really have to know what elements are related to you. In my case, instead of thinking of a mélange or a synthesis of east-west culture, I'm thinking of an interaction between the interior self and various cultures."[14]

Ung has composed a variety of chamber works, including the series *Spiral I* through *Spiral VII*, and larger orchestral pieces such as *Inner Voices* and *Triple Concerto*. Ung is also a solo instrumentalist, preserving Cambodian culture through performances on the Cambodian xylophone. He explains that his desire to preserve his country's culture motivates him: "The reason that I have been doing that is because I want to maintain or to sustain Cambodian cultural elements after the holocaust. We lost about two million people, so we had gathered artists and intellectuals and tried to reconstruct the culture one more time. I promised myself not to mix what I am doing on the Cambodian xylophone as to accompany the classical dance of Cambodia with what I am writing for essentially western instruments. However, it is one person doing both things, and you can not really avoid certain infiltration here and there. When it comes, I suppose it comes naturally."[15]

During his month-long residency at the Atlantic Center for the Arts, Ung worked with eight associate artists who were selected from applicants from across the United States. Ung says the natural surroundings of the Atlantic Center provide him and his students with the perfect state of mind to compose music. While at the center, Ung gave a series of seminars to his associates, covering such topics as imagination in composing, the concept of musical time, and the artistic fingerprint.

In addition to discussing musical concepts with the associate artists, Ung offered constructive comments about pieces composed by them: "They have been bringing their musical sketches to me, and I have helped them out. It is not my intention to interfere with what they are doing; it is just to help them to see their sketches as clear as possible. My analogy for the student-instructor relationship is this. It's like a triangle, with the left point as the student, the right point is the instructor, and the top point is the sketch that is being presented. A sketch, to represent it in metaphor, is almost like a shattered mirror. What I'm trying to do is encourage the student to put this shattered mirror together, to the point where he or she can see himself or herself. That is my job. When they have mastered that, they can do whatever they want. They can throw that mirror through the window and make it shatter, either by random, or organize the debris and put it back together to make artistic sense."[16]

Like many of the resident artists at the Atlantic Center, Ung also took advantage of the serene, natural setting to compose his own work when he was not giving instruction to his associates.

Although the Atlantic Center encourages interdisciplinary collaborations among the various artists in residence, the center occasionally hosts a residency with three master artists from the same discipline. One such project brought together poet Diane Di Prima, novelist Bebe Moore Campbell, and playwright Jack Gelber for a writers' residency.

Poet Diane Di Prima has been a serious writer since she was fourteen years old. She was a leader of the Beat movement in the 1950s and 1960s and has written more than thirty books of poetry. Di Prima founded the Poet's Press and cofounded the New York Poet's Theater. Di Prima explains how she selected the group of associate artists she worked with at the Atlantic Center: "I was looking for people who had a good ear for the poem, for the line, but I was also looking for people who had some sense of a breadth

A boardwalk winds through the Atlantic Center for the Arts, connecting the studios and artists' residences. Playwright Edward Albee, cellist Mstislav Rostropovich, and sculptor Duane Hanson are just some of the many world-famous artists to be in residence at the Atlantic Center for the Arts.

of point of view, a largeness of point of view, or some kind of background vision for their work. Even if you're writing the most simple domestic poem, you must also see yourself as part of humanity as a whole in some way, instead of just locked into a small thing. That's also something I work on with people, that we open up more, and let more of the world in that we're writing about. I was also looking for people who had some excitement for writing, who really cared about it."[17]

Bebe Moore Campbell is a novelist and journalist, who also does commentary for the National Public Radio program *Morning Edition*. Campbell wrote the novels *Your Blues Ain't Like Mine* and *Sweet Summer: Growing Up with and without My Dad*. Campbell's work has also been published in the *New York Times Magazine* and *Book Review*. At the Atlantic Center, Campbell was instructing her associates on the art of writing a novel. While at the Center, Campbell said it was the perfect setting to study the arts, surrounded by water and trees. She said she would like to see similar facilities built to serve urban youth: "My first impression when I came here was a fervent wish that I could one day create something like this for kids in the inner city to come and have a chance to perhaps discover their talents. To be taken from their environment and be placed into one where they could try different things. Photography, music, writing, drama, dance. I think it would be so beneficial to those kids who don't have this kind of opportunity."[18]

Jack Gelber is a playwright and director who has won many awards for his off-Broadway productions. He teaches college in Brooklyn and conducted play-writing workshops for mid-career artists at the Atlantic Center. He describes his workshops: "My students come in with their work, we read it, we try to figure out what it's all about, how it's working, whether it's as effective as the student wants it to be, and what can be done to make it a better play."[19] Gelber says that all the plays his associates brought to the Atlantic Center were very different, and that each playwright had unique concerns and needs: "The one thing that binds us all together is the difficulty of being a playwright in our country. It's not an occupation that is in great demand, all over the country. We struggle to get productions and we try to share information about who's doing what, and who likes what, and where to go, and possibly who to write or talk to get some work on, both on a community level, perhaps a regional level, New York, or wherever."[20]

In 1993, the Atlantic Center for the Arts began participating in a project-oriented residency called Music in Motion. The project is cosponsored by the Atlantic Center and the Relache Music Ensemble of Philadelphia. The project is held in three-year cycles at five residency sites around the country: Phoenix, Seattle, Minneapolis, Philadelphia, and New Smyrna Beach. At each residency, a musical ensemble is placed with two composers. The idea is that the ensemble and the composers will collaborate on two new pieces of music, which will eventually be presented to the public. The ensembles and composers in each residency are brought together for one week, three times a year. The final residency includes a presentation in which a finished piece, or something close to a finished piece, is given a public performance.

Executive Director Suzanne Fetcher says that some interesting experimental works are coming out of the Music In Motion residencies: "The whole project is really geared toward two things: collaborating on new music and building audiences for new music, so outreach is a significant component to each of these residencies. Audiences are invited in to experience an open rehearsal format where the composers and the ensemble will interact with the audience and describe to them the creative process. They become more aware what that particular composer is thinking about, when he or she is composing a piece of work, what the influences are, what the instrumentation might suggest. Then we try to bring the same audiences back for each of the residencies so they see the development and hear the development of the piece, so that they really are a part of the creative process. At the final presentation residency for that year, they hear the final piece, the finished piece, and they feel really invested in the whole process. I think that when it comes to work that might be sort of abstract and not necessarily lyrical, that this sort of presentation brings people in and makes the music so much more accessible than would otherwise really be possible."[21]

In an effort to allow the master artists and their associates to be even more productive while in residence at the Atlantic Center for the Arts, the facility broke ground on a $3.1-million expansion in the summer of 1994, which was completed in 1996. In addition to the administration building, artist housing, two common work areas, and an outdoor performance space already available at the center, discipline-specific work spaces were created. The expansion includes a music studio with recording equipment available, a dance studio, a sculpture studio, an indoor black-box theater with 250 seats, a painting studio, a library, and a newly renovated dining hall.

The new buildings were designed to blend with the existing unobtrusive, modern wooden structures of the center, which are all connected with a series of elevated wooden walkways. The dense foliage surrounding the Atlantic Center hides the fact that the buildings are close together, keeping the intrusion on the natural surroundings to a minimum. The close proximity of the discipline-specific work spaces also encourages interaction among the various disciplines. The new structures, designed by Thompson and Rose Architects of Cambridge, Massachusetts, have been well received, winning the 1993 Boston Society of Architects Award.

Architect Charles Rose says he wanted the new Atlantic Center buildings to be functional and attractive, and not to disrupt the natural setting of the facility: "This is an indigenous, natural site, which we find to be wonderful, and feels sort of like a remnant of an earlier vegetal state in Florida. The weaving boardwalk gives you a very peripatetic sense of space, and we've also tried to scale the buildings in such a way that they're not overpowering, and have a similar scale to the buildings that are already there at the center."[22]

Rose adds that the artistic purpose of each building was taken into account when it was designed. For example, the studios to be used by visual artists were designed to avoid direct sunlight, with louvered windows, drawing on earlier climatic architectural techniques used in Florida. The interior of the theater studio was designed with an enclosed matte black finish, to allow experimental theater to be performed. The interiors of the buildings are not to compete with the art that will be produced there: "All of the buildings on the outside are sculpturally interesting, and the exterior composition really establishes a clear, modern, and new language, but the interiors are purposefully left blank, in a way, so that the spaces can be really occupied and filled by the creating artists there."[23]

In addition to hosting four to six artist residencies a year, the Atlantic Center for the Arts operates the Harris House Gallery in downtown New Smyrna Beach and sponsors an annual juried art show of works by artists in Florida's state university system. Atlantic Center's founder Doris Leeper says that the expansion of the facility allows more community outreach projects: "I think it gives us an opportunity to do a lot of things we haven't been able to do before. As an example, we had a very crude space for dance, and now we have a wonderful studio coming on line for that. We had no indoor theater space, very limited space within the existing workshop, where we could seat maybe a hundred or a hundred and twenty-five people max, and we can seat about two hundred and fifty in the new theater.

"There's just a lot of things that are possible that weren't possible before. When we started, we just had the one building, the Whatmore workshop, where everything had to take place, and it was pretty tight. We think the expansion is going to be really positive. Our downtown satellite, Harris House, can expand its program for the community. Again, they had no way to do dance or theater for their children's and adult programs. The kids are going to have a really wonderful opportunity. We think the facility, when completed, with all six new buildings, is probably going to be the best artist community facility in this country, and possibly in the world."[24]

Although Leeper is best known as the founder of the Atlantic Center for the Arts, she is also well respected as an artist in her own right. On the same weekend that the first phase of the Atlantic Center's expansion was opened to the public in the fall of 1995, two separate exhibitions of Leeper's work were displayed in Central Florida.

"Doris Leeper: A Retrospective" opened at the Cornell Fine Arts Museum at Rollins College, featuring fifty-three paintings and sculptures from Leeper's four-and-a-half-decade career. Since much of Leeper's work is large-scale site-specific sculpture that cannot be moved, the exhibition featured twenty-two photographs of those pieces. Three new outdoor sculptures by Leeper were also unveiled.

On the same day that the retrospective exhibition opened at Cornell, the Albertson-Peterson Gallery in Winter Park opened "Doris Leeper: New Dimensions, 1995." That exhibition featured all new works by Leeper, which were smaller sculptures combining natural and created elements. Most of Leeper's work as an artist utilizes a combination of geometric shapes, especially the triangle. Her best-known work is *Steel Quilt*, a large sculpture permanently on display at the Orlando International Airport.

With all the time Leeper had to put into creating the Atlantic Center for the Arts, she is pleased that her work as an artist is not being forgotten: "The Atlantic Center really took the great majority of my time for a whole decade, and a little bit before and since then. I was fairly well along in identity as a successful artist when I started the center, and I've said to myself a million times, 'Will I ever get back to where I was before?' and I've also wondered if, when I have full time to do my work again, which I do now, will the work be as significant as the work I was doing. We'll have to see what the response is to the new work. If I had my druthers, I'd rather be thought of as an artist than someone who came up with a grand idea. I agree Atlantic Center is a wonderful project, but my interest is in producing work."[25]

The lasting significance of Doris Leeper's work as an artist will be determined by future generations. What is clear now, however, is that Doris Leeper's artistic vision has made and will continue to make a lasting contribution to Central Florida culture through the Atlantic Center for the Arts. The Atlantic Center stands as a constant reminder of the importance of preserving Florida's natural environment, as well as the necessity of looking at art in new ways, and exploring collaboration within different disciplines of the arts. With the newly expanded facilities, the Atlantic Center is able to reach out to an even larger portion of the Central Florida community, and the work accomplished there will continue to reach an international and culturally diverse audience.

✳ The Space Coast

A Bridge between the Past and the Future

Florida's Space Coast includes the towns of Satellite Beach, Indian Harbour Beach, Indialantic, Eau Gallie, Merritt Island, Rockledge, historic Titusville, and the cultural havens Cocoa and Melbourne, which are all in close proximity to the John F. Kennedy Space Center at Cape Canaveral. The Space Coast area of Brevard County is unique because it celebrates both the indigenous and pioneer cultures of the past, while supporting scientific and exploratory programs that may be the key to the future of humankind.

The earliest residents of the Space Coast were the Ais Indians, an ancient tribe that predates the Seminoles, but also coexisted with them in Central Florida. It is believed that the Ais lived in east Central Florida as early as the Ice Age. When the Spanish began colonizing Florida in the late 1500s, they established a fort on the Space Coast called Santa Lucinda and enslaved the Ais. Many Ais fled the Spanish oppression, but the tribe was essentially extinct by 1600. Most of the remaining Ais were probably absorbed into the Seminole tribe in the early seventeenth century.[1]

While living on the Space Coast, the Spanish planted orange groves that flourished in Central Florida's comfortable climate. The Spanish abandoned Fort Lucinda, and when the British began settling in Florida, they labeled the Space Coast "unconquerable." With the Ais driven out, the Spanish gone, and the lack of interest on the part of the British, the only living things on Florida's Space Coast in the late 1700s and early 1800s were plants and wildlife.

Efforts to preserve the memory of the early inhabitants of the Space Coast are under way. Exhibitions at the Brevard County Historical Museum look at the culture of the Ais and the early Spanish settlers. The Cocoa campus of Brevard Community College hosts an annual Seminole Indian and Pioneer Festival in late September that attracts tens of thousands of people to demonstrations of Native American dancing, storytelling, craft work, and cooking. The lifestyles of Central Florida's early white settlers are also explored at the festival.

In 1993 the Storytellers of Brevard expanded their repertoire to include an annual theatrical presentation called Into the Wind. The program changes and evolves from year to year but always focuses on Native American legends, music, and dancing. Thousands of Central Florida schoolchildren are bused to the Cocoa Village Playhouse every year to see the program, which is also presented in performances open to the public.

Into the Wind was created by Gail Ryan, the founder and artistic director of the Storytellers of Brevard. Ryan was inspired to develop Into the Wind after attending a Native American powwow: "At that point my life completely changed in my concept of the spirituality of the Native American. I finally met a Native American here in the community, Mr. Omi, and then I read a great deal about the Native American, so that I would have a comprehension. I'm ashamed to say that my knowledge was so minute, and yet here I was a graduate student who had taught thirty-six years, humanities at the college level, and I knew nothing about this marvelous cultural face of our country that has been here for thousands of years. I found out through the Native American myths and legends that they have a way of addressing all problems that we meet as human beings, not just as Native Americans, but as human beings. They have a largeness to the story which is unique, that can cause growth in a human being when they hear it."[2]

With dramatic lighting, special effects, music, and dancing accompanying the storytelling, Into the Wind brings to life Native American myths and legends about how various animals acquired their characteristics and how natural phenomena like wind and the cycle of day and night originated and tales of tolerance for and acceptance of others. The use of authentic costumes and instruments, as well as Native American cast members, adds credibility to the performances.

Kenneth Omi, a Native American who regularly appears in the annual productions of Into theWind and has helped to shape the content of the program, explains its purpose: "I believe it serves two purposes. It educates the public, which is the non-Indian population, about the philosophies and traditions of the Native Americans, but it has also drawn the Native Americans together also. We're getting to know each other, and sometimes their opinions are taken into account in the way we make presentations. I think future productions are going to rely pretty much on an increased involvement from the outside, and we welcome that. I think these presentations we are doing are allowing us to do two things, address the non-Indian as well as the Native American populations."[3]

In recent decades some younger Native Americans have reportedly been losing interest in preserving their heritage. Traditional music, dance, and storytelling have had difficulty competing with modern pop culture. Kenneth Omi says programs like Into the Wind help to reverse that trend and revitalize Native American children's interest in the history and traditions of their people, contributing to a sense of community: "There might have been that trend, but I know that the trend is changing. There are now many organizations that are helping the Native American to realize their culture—that is the relationship of nature with man—and a lot of their education and a lot of their projects are focused in on that, bringing man and the environment back together again. As Native Americans we find Into the Wind very valuable, because it's a way that information can be disseminated among other peoples, and we know that it can be preserved in that way."[4]

Following the departure of Native Americans and the Spanish from the Space Coast, the area was sporadically inhabited until the late 1800s. After the United States took control of Florida in 1821, pirates frequently attacked American ships in the waters off the Space Coast. In 1843, a brick lighthouse was built at Cape Canaveral to help ships navigate. The lighthouse was manned by Captain Mills Olcott Burnham, who started a pineapple plantation near Cocoa Beach. In the mid-1800s many families came to settle on the Space Coast but few stayed. During the Civil War the lighthouse was dismantled, and most families moved away from the area.[5]

The longest-lasting early settlement in the Space Coast area was started by a family of freed slaves following the Civil War. The homesteaders claimed all of the land south of Cape Canaveral, between the Banana River and the Atlantic Ocean. In 1885 a hurricane hit the coast, flooding out the homesteaders, but ten years later the town of Cocoa was settled on the mainland.[6]

Among the activities to commemorate the centennial of Cocoa in 1995 was the establishment of the annual Cocoa Village Jazz Festival. The use of jazz to celebrate the town's one hundredth birthday was particularly appropriate since jazz is also said to have been created in 1895. In coming years the festival will continue to galvanize the community spirit on the Space Coast through the enjoyment of American music. Jeff Simpson organized the Cocoa Village Jazz Festival held in March 1995. He describes the purpose of the festival: "What we hope to achieve is to bring a broader cultural horizon to the Space Coast by pulling together all of the different peoples

The historic Cocoa Village Playhouse, a vaudeville theater in the early twentieth century and a movie house in the mid twentieth century, is currently the stage for locally produced plays, musicals, and other live performances. The theater is on Brevard Avenue in Cocoa, the site of many historic buildings and outdoor arts and crafts festivals.

from the north end of the county to the south end of the county, from all the way to Orlando to come over and congregate for a big outdoor celebration of American music. Whether or not it's true that jazz was founded in 1895, that's the date designated, and it coincides with the centennial of Cocoa village."[7]

People continued to settle on the Space Coast throughout the early twentieth century, and gradually the communities that still exist today were established. The Florida land boom of the 1920s had an impact on the area, and the most well preserved examples of the architecture from that period can be found on Brevard Avenue in Cocoa and on East New Haven Avenue in Melbourne. While each street has its own unique characteristics, the ambience of Brevard Avenue and East New Haven Avenue is similar to that of Park Avenue in Winter Park and Donnelly Street in Mount Dora.

The city of Titusville, located just across the Indian River from the Kennedy Space Center, also has an impressive historic district. Twenty-four

The Myles Building, constructed in 1913, is on East New Haven Avenue in Melbourne. The building originally housed a billiard hall and the Midway Hotel, but it has also been the offices of the *Melbourne Times* newspaper and temporary classrooms in the early twentieth century. It is believed that gangster Al Capone played pool here following Prohibition.

buildings in downtown Titusville are listed on the National Register of Historic Places. Colonel Henry Titus founded Titusville in 1867 on an undeveloped piece of land. By the time the town was incorporated in 1887, it had a post office, a newspaper, two hotels, several businesses, and a population of four hundred. In 1895, a fire destroyed much of downtown Titusville, but many buildings from the late nineteenth and early twentieth centuries still stand today.

The most significant period of development on the Space Coast began in 1939 with the construction of the Banana River Naval Air Station. The presence of the Navy brought more people to the Space Coast. In 1941 the State Road 520 causeway was built, replacing a wooden bridge from the mainland to the peninsula, which increased tourism in the area. During World War II German submarines sank American freighters off the coast, and local residents kept a lookout for enemy airplanes. In 1948 the Banana River Naval Air Station was converted to Patrick Air Force Base, and a missile program was initiated.[8]

The Emma Parrish Theater, built in 1905, is the cultural center of Titusville. Currently the home of the Titusville Playhouse, the building has also been used as a saloon, a pool hall, a silent movie house, and apartments. After restoring the building in the early 1980s, the Titusville Playhouse began presenting a full season of musicals and plays here.

In 1949, President Harry Truman established a long-range proving ground for missiles at Cape Canaveral. The coordinated activities of the government stations at Cape Canaveral and Patrick Air Force Base swelled the population of the Space Coast. By 1959 the newly formed National Aeronautics and Space Administration was successfully launching lunar probes from Cape Canaveral, which eventually led to the manned exploration of space. Central Florida became the launch point for NASA's exploratory and scientific missions in space.[9]

Population statistics from the 1950s illustrate the impact that Patrick Air Force Base and NASA had on the Space Coast. From 1950 to 1960, the population of Florida grew by 78.7 percent, from 2.8 million to 4.9 million. During that same period the population of Brevard County expanded by 371.1 percent, from 23,000 to 111,435.[10]

The dramatic increase in the population of the Space Coast in the second half of the twentieth century led to the establishment of a wide variety of performing arts and cultural organizations to serve the area. The Surfside Players, the Civic Theater of Melbourne, and the Brevard Symphony Orchestra are among the groups that were created during this period. In 1975 the Brevard Cultural Alliance was founded to serve as the arts and cultural affairs council of Brevard County, promoting arts and cultural endeavors, arts education, and economic development through cultural tourism. Kay Elliot Burke, executive director of the Brevard Cultural Alliance, describes the members of the alliance: "We have about forty-five really viable, actively programming organizations, and probably another thirty-five or forty that function on a part-time basis, meeting one specific programmatic need. Our larger organizations include two symphony orchestras that serve our community; we have an art museum with a children's science museum component; we have a history museum; we have five community theater organizations, one theater organization that is primarily an Equity Actor's program. We have a variety of art leagues or artists' groups that are very busy in our community and provide arts programming on a regular basis. We have about twenty-six festivals that take place in our community throughout the year, and among those are the Space Coast Art Festival, the Melbourne Art Festival, and a variety of other community arts and cultural festivals. There's one going on at least every month, and usually two, sometimes three."[11]

The art festivals and performing arts institutions on the Space Coast help to bring together the sometimes fractured communities of Brevard County as arts and cultural programs are prone to do. As Kay Elliot Burke explains, artistic efforts help to bridge geographic boundaries, as well as imagined class distinctions between people in various economic and social groups: "The arts and cultural groups in Brevard County help to promote a sense of community by having active community participation in our programs. We have a very strong volunteer base of support for our different groups. The cultural institutions and programs become gathering places for community members. As they work together to produce a program, it builds a sense of community.

"We have managed to cross some geographic and parochial boundary lines through the arts in Brevard County that the rest of the community has yet to accomplish. Our community, outside the arts, views itself as north, central, and south, and then there's the mainland and the beaches. Some boundaries are caused by natural geographic things such as the rivers and the ocean. It divides the county in ways that you can physically see, as well as just some geographic parochialism that exists. There are strong sentiments about north, central, and south, in a variety of business organizations and others. In the arts, we realized many years ago that we are one community.

"Our county is seventy-two miles long, and it takes almost two hours to travel from one end to the other. We realized that if we didn't learn to gather centrally at least once a month to discuss matters of interest, and work together as an arts and cultural community, that we would get decimated in the political and business support processes. I think the arts teach us all how to communicate a little better, and so it makes sense to me that the arts groups and artists communicate across those imaginary or geographic boundaries."[12]

While the arts and cultural organizations in Brevard County have undoubtedly helped to contribute to a sense of community in the area, the arts groups there have not been without their own incidents of divisiveness. For example, when musicians in the Brevard Symphony Orchestra were displeased with their management, some of them left the group in 1985 to form the Space Coast Philharmonic (which was later renamed the

Space Coast Pops). Although the two orchestras were initially perceived as competitors, they now peacefully coexist and serve two different functions in the community. Christopher Confessore, the music director and principal conductor of the Brevard Symphony Orchestra, mentions some of the differences between the two orchestras: "Judging from the types of programs that they do and when they put them on, I think we're sort of serving two different audiences. They seem to be putting their concerts on Sunday afternoons, and at least a couple of the programs I've seen seem to be pops or lighter oriented, and that's great. I know there's some past history from nine or ten years ago that I was not around for, but I suppose that since both orchestras have coexisted for ten years, I guess it seems to be going okay."[13]

Candler Schaffer, the music director and principal conductor of the Space Coast Pops, agrees that Brevard County's two orchestras are more complementary than competitive: "Well, both orchestras are very fine orchestras. I have played in both orchestras myself as a musician, and actually most of the musicians are separate for each orchestra, and the audiences are separate audiences, and to some extent I think that the programming is also separate. So really I think that we can all coexist peacefully. There's enough music in the world for everybody. Also, in a way, I think competition is good because it keeps people making sure that they're playing their music as good as they can, and I think that's good."[14]

Together with Disney World, and more recently the Orlando Magic basketball team, the activities of NASA have brought world-wide attention to Central Florida. NASA's efforts on the Space Coast have made Central Florida a significant site of crucial developments in human history. All of America's manned missions in space have departed from the John F. Kennedy Space Center at Cape Canaveral.

The space program's galvanizing effect on the Central Florida community can be witnessed by the thousands of people who pack the highways near Cape Canaveral every time a manned spacecraft is launched and by the large numbers of people who step outside of their homes and offices throughout the area, just to catch a glimpse of the space shuttle's exhaust trail.

Among the many important NASA missions launched from Central Florida is the first United States manned spaceflight of Alan B. Shepard in

1961, and John H. Glenn's orbit of the earth the following year. In 1969 Neil Armstrong became the first person to walk on the moon after departing the spacecraft that he boarded in Central Florida. The first reusable spacecraft, the space shuttle Columbia, was launched from Cape Canaveral in 1981 and many shuttle missions have followed.

Milestones of NASA's Central Florida–based space shuttle program include the 1983 mission that made Sally K. Ride the first American woman astronaut to travel in space, and the 1984 mission that allowed Kathryn D. Sullivan to become the first woman to walk in space. In 1986 tragedy struck the space program as the space shuttle Challenger exploded moments after takeoff, killing the crew, which included civilian teacher Christa McAuliffe.

It took two years for NASA to regroup following the Challenger disaster, with space shuttle launches resuming in 1988. That year Dave Pignanelli, a reporter based at 90.7 WMFE in Orlando, began covering the space program for National Public Radio. Pignanelli has witnessed more than fifty space shuttle launches from Cape Canaveral but says he never tires of them: "It's truly a thrill to be there, to feel the grandstand where the media sit

The Shuttle of Tomorrow is on permanent display outside the Astronaut Hall of Fame at the Kennedy Space Center in Cape Canaveral. All of NASA's manned spaceflights have been launched from Central Florida, including the 1969 Apollo mission that took Neil Armstrong to the moon.

shake when the roar of the shuttle engines comes our way; it's truly a thrill. You'd have to be a robot not to get caught up in the thrill of watching a launch, regardless of how many times you've seen it. Night launches are the most exciting because during the first three seconds of the launch, when the engines ignite and the shuttle is just a foot or two off the launch pad, it's like daylight for a brief instant at the Kennedy Space Center. If it's real cloudy, the light is reflected off the clouds, and it's even brighter."[15]

Pignanelli's enthusiasm for the space shuttle program is matched by people throughout Central Florida—and the world. Visitors to the John F. Kennedy Space Center can enjoy exhibitions chronicling the history of manned spaceflight at Spaceport USA and at the Astronaut Hall of Fame. Guided tours of NASA's launch pads are also available.

The communities of the Space Coast are preserving the cultural heritage of Central Florida by actively celebrating the area's earliest inhabitants, by recognizing the founding of communities that still exist today, and by serving as the launching pad of the future of humankind.

Conclusion

Central Florida is experiencing consistent growth and evolution. The booming tourism industry is spawning the development of new attractions, as well as the expansion of the existing theme parks. The uninitiated traveler can easily pass by Zora Neale Hurston's Eatonville, André Smith's Maitland, and Charles Hosmer Morse's Winter Park in a matter of seconds on Interstate 4. What used to be sleepy towns are now bustling segments of the greater Orlando area. Even the formerly remote town of Christmas and other long-time rural communities are being swallowed up in new homes, shopping centers, schools, and businesses.

Feelings of alienation and the lack of a sense of community accompany Central Florida's seemingly unrestrained growth. Residents are longing for a strong tie to the area and are looking for ways to perceive the region they live in as home. Cultural and historic preservation efforts in Central Florida can help to stimulate feelings of pride and belonging among residents in the area.

Many tourists are happy to limit their vacations to the experiences that they can have at Disney World, Sea World, and Universal Studios, but others would enjoy expanding their Central Florida visits to include outings of historical and cultural significance. While few people would expect a family trip to Mount Dora or Cocoa to eclipse a visit to Disney World, an afternoon in either town could provide a relaxing yet stimulating day trip to augment a theme park vacation.

Central Florida is in a unique position to benefit from the growing interest in cultural and heritage tourism. With more than 40 million visitors coming to the area every year, the promotion of opportunities beyond a theme park visit could have a significant economic impact. In 1997, Florida's Ecotourism/Heritage Tourism Advisory Committee determined: "By preserving our unique resources, we have the best opportunity to maintain our position as the number one tourist destination in the world by offering a well-rounded array of visitor opportunities that appeal to many tastes and foster repeat visitation. By promoting our unique natural, cultural and historic assets we have the best opportunity to generate the financial resources and the broad-based understanding that will be needed to protect them."[1]

The most significant way that future generations will be able to feel a deep and lasting tie to the Central Florida community is through the historic preservation projects of the present. Efforts to maintain historic buildings and participation in active cultural celebrations like the Zora Neale Hurston Festival of the Arts and Humanities must be encouraged and stimulated. The tourism industry will benefit from these efforts as well, because visitors will have a wider range of vacation options while in Central Florida.

N. Y. Nathiri, director of the Association to Preserve the Eatonville Community, says that historic preservation efforts are often misunderstood: "We preservationists have a tough row to hoe because people say, 'Oh yes, they don't want to just stop progress, they want to go back to the 1880s and the 1900s!' As a matter of fact, it's a bum rap, and we have to fight it. When I say 'we,' I mean preservationists have to fight it collectively. This is what we were saying back in 1987, when we first got organized—that for future development, for the growth, for the planned growth, for the quality growth of the Eatonville community, historic preservation is the hook, it is the idea, it is the concept that will allow this community to move forward. I say that without any hesitation, given all that we have been able to learn. We are in the mainstream vision of preservation for the twenty-first century."[2]

Other Central Florida communities could learn a lot from Eatonville's example. Ethnic celebrations like the Florida Irish Festival, Fiesta Medina, and the Orlando Carnival Caribbean Festival are prevalent in Central Florida, and events like the Winter Park Sidewalk Art Festival, the Orlando International Fringe Festival, and the Florida Film Festival offer a variety of annual cultural experiences. The Zora Neale Hurston Festival of the Arts and Humanities, held the last week of January, stands apart, however, as the best example of how the cultural heritage of Central Florida can be exploited in a positive way.

Many theater companies, dance troupes, musical organizations, art galleries, and historical museums present exciting programs in the area throughout the year. Gary Libby, director of the Museum of Arts and Sciences in Daytona Beach and president of the Florida Art Museum Directors Association, points out that arts institutions often preserve local history for residents and visitors, promoting a sense of community, even when that is not their primary mission: "Cultural organizations are in the forefront of organizations who use history by revisiting some of the great moments of our past as lessons for the future, in an attempt to suggest that we are a unique community. Florida is a very new state, 1845 is statehood, and it wasn't until after the Second World War when Florida really experienced a huge boom in population. It's very easy for many Floridians to forget that Florida itself has an integrity and a past. Cultural organizations at their very core are interested in not only the past as a denominator of the strength of a community, but also in how the present becomes the past, and becomes something that binds communities together.

"Orlando is a very good example of a very new city that's writing its own history in very strong and bold terms right now, probably more dramatically than any other city in the state. Areas like Daytona Beach are also developing a sense of the importance of history, not only as an adjunct of economic development with historic tourism, but also as the gum that tends to bind us together as people, as just humans. I think you'll see in Florida, probably, as we head toward the year 2000, a renewed interest in the historic past, and how we can make history important for Floridians in the future."[3]

The preservation of historically significant buildings also strengthens the sense of community in Central Florida by allowing individual towns to retain a sense of identity. The historic preservation efforts underway in Sanford, DeLand, and Mount Dora demonstrate to other area towns how older buildings can create a colorful ambience. The restoration and protection of historic buildings and homes give the Central Florida community a unique character, which is attractive to both tourists and residents.

While many significant buildings have been lost locally, Orlando Mayor Glenda Hood feels strongly about the importance of historic preservation: "When people come to this community, they want to come and learn the history of our community. They look for those exhibits, those places that they can visit. Think about when you go to another city. Why do you go there? You go there for something that's related to culture—its history, its museums, its special exhibits—it's the ambience, the environment within the community. Culture in the broadest sense includes those things. The architectural style, the parks, the environment, the natural beauty. In our community, expanding on that, it includes our attractions, it includes other types of experiences that we can have here. So we want to make sure that we continue to offer all of the above for our residents and our visitors alike."[4]

Sara Van Arsdel, executive director of the Orange County Historical Society, is a leading protector of the cultural heritage of Central Florida. The Orange County Historical Museum exhibits local artifacts, collects oral histories, and encourages the preservation of historic buildings. Van Arsdel is cautiously optimistic about the future of historic preservation in Central Florida. "You're always going to have, tragically and sadly, some losses. On the other hand, there's still a lot of things out there. I do believe that as people hear more about historic preservation projects and, again, how this really helps to build the fabric of the community and is what makes a community unique—I think that when they know and they understand, then they appreciate. I look at it as an uphill battle, but I'm very optimistic about the future of history."[5]

The growth and expansion of the city of Orlando and its nearby towns into a major metropolitan area is inevitable. What can be controlled is how that growth is allowed to occur, and how the history of the area is maintained and celebrated. Only through the enjoyment and preservation of the cultural heritage of Central Florida will future generations be able to look at the area and see anything of significance beyond the theme parks.

Appendix A

Central Florida's Arts and Cultural Organizations

The Acting Studio Company (407)425-2281
952 South Orange Avenue
Orlando, Florida 32806
Presents a series of plays throughout the year. Also conducts acting classes and workshops.

Albertson-Peterson Gallery (407)628-1258
329 Park Avenue
Winter Park, Florida 32789-4390
Displays rotating exhibits of contemporary art throughout the year.

Albin Polášek Museum (407)647-6294
633 Osceola Avenue
Winter Park, Florida 32789-4429
Sculpture and paintings by Albin Polášek are on permanent display.

Alice and William Jenkins Gallery at Crealde School of Art
(407)671-1886
600 St. Andrews Boulevard
Winter Park, Florida 32789
Presents student and professional visual-art exhibits.

Altamonte Jazz Ensemble, Inc. (407)322-7528
119 Bent Oak Court
Sanford, Florida 32773
Presents three free concerts a year to perpetuate an appreciation for big-band jazz.

American Guild of Organists (904)734-1087
204 West Stetson Avenue
DeLand, Florida 32720
A national organization dedicated to promoting organ and choral music.
Presents recitals and concerts throughout the year.

Annie Russell Theater (407)646-2145
Rollins College
1000 Holt Avenue
Winter Park, Florida 32789-3325
Presents five plays a year and hosts visiting performances.

Artists League of Orange County (407)849-0840 ext. 254
6903 Sugarbush Lane
Orlando, Florida 32819
Presents at least one visual-art show a year for member artists,
and continuing exhibits at various locations.

Arts on Douglas (904)428-1133
123 Douglas Street
New Smyrna Beach, Florida 32168-7137
Displays artwork by fifty Florida artists throughout the year
and hosts guest exhibits.

Asian Cultural Association (407)333-3667
2759 Marsh Wren Circle
Longwood, Florida 32779
Promotes the preservation of ancient Asian performing arts traditions.
Presents concerts, dance recitals, films, visual-art exhibits, and student
workshops throughout the year.

Association to Preserve the Eatonville Community
(407)647-3307
227 East Kennedy Boulevard
Eatonville, Florida 32751
Promotes historic preservation in Eatonville. Presents the annual Zora Neale
Hurston Festival of the Arts and Humanities in January, the Summer
Performing Arts Workshop for Children and Youth, Institutes for Teachers,

and year-round visual-art exhibits in the Zora Neale Hurston National Museum of Fine Arts.

Atlantic Center for the Arts (904)427-6975
1414 Art Center Avenue
New Smyrna Beach, Florida 32168-5560
Hosts several master artist residencies a year, which culminate in public performances. Also exhibits visual art throughout the year and operates the Harris House Gallery.

Authors in the Park (407)658-4520
P.O. Box 85
Winter Park, Florida 32790-0085
Sponsors an annual short-story contest. Winners are published in the journal Fine Print.

Bach Festival Society of Winter Park (407)646-2182
1000 Holt Avenue—2763
Winter Park, Florida 32789
Presents the annual Winter Park Bach Festival in late February and early March, as well as concerts throughout the year as part of the Festival Concert Series.

Bay Street Players (904)357-7777
State Theater
109 North Bay Street
Eustis, Florida 32726-3402
Presents six theatrical performances a year in the State Theater.

Brevard Museum of Art and Science (407)242-0737
1520 Highland Avenue
Melbourne, Florida 32935-6521
Presents rotating visual-art exhibits throughout the year.

Brevard Museum of History and Science (407)632-1830
2201 Michigan Avenue
Cocoa, Florida 32926-5618
Presents exhibits of artifacts from Central Florida history.

Brevard Symphony Orchestra (407)242-2024
1500 Highland Avenue
Melbourne, Florida 32935-6521
Presents a series of classical music concerts throughout the year at the King Center for the Performing Arts and other venues.

Camerata Chorus (407)426-1717
111 North Orange Avenue
Orlando, Florida 32801
The chorus of the Orlando Opera Company. Also presents several choral concerts throughout the year.

Casements Cultural Center (904)676-3216
25 Riverside Drive
Ormond Beach, Florida 32176-6520
Presents rotating visual-art exhibits throughout the year.

Cathedral Series (407)849-0680
Cathedral Church of St. Luke
P.O. Box 2328
Orlando, Florida 32802
Presents a series of classical music concerts at the Cathedral Church of St. Luke in downtown Orlando, and the Bach's Lunch series.

Celebration Players (407)528-3588
510 Campus Street
Celebration, Florida 34747
Presents plays, musicals, and children's theater works throughout the year.

Center Players (407)645-5933
851 North Maitland Avenue
Maitland, Florida 32751
Located at the Jewish Community Center. Presents several theatrical performances a year.

Central Florida Cultural Endeavors (904) 257-7790
201 University Boulevard
Daytona Beach, Florida 32118-3752
*Presents a series of chamber music concerts throughout the year
at Our Lady of Lourdes Church.*

Central Florida Dance Theater Performing Arts Group
(407) 273-4017
1600 Park Manor Drive
Orlando, Florida 32825
Presents student dance concerts of ballet, jazz, and tap.

Charles Hosmer Morse Museum of American Art
(407) 645-5311
445 Park Avenue North
Winter Park, Florida 32789
*Exhibits American art, including an extensive collection of work
by stained-glass artist Louis Comfort Tiffany.*

Civic Theater of Central Florida (407) 896-7365
1001 East Princeton Street
Orlando, Florida 32803-1420
*Presents a wide variety of plays throughout the year, including the Main
Stage, Second Stage, and Family Classics series. Offers workshops through
the Civic School of Theater Arts.*

Cocoa Village Playhouse (407) 636-5050
300 Brevard Avenue
Cocoa, Florida 32922-7969
*Presents a series of plays and musicals throughout the year, and hosts
performances by groups such as the Storytellers of Brevard.*

The Cornell Fine Arts Museum (407) 646-2526
Rollins College
1000 Holt Avenue
Winter Park, Florida 32789
*Presents visual-art exhibits. The museum has an extensive permanent
collection and presents touring exhibits.*

Crealde School of Visual Art (407) 671-1886
600 St. Andrews Boulevard
Winter Park, Florida 32792
Offers studio classes in ceramics, sculpture, painting and drawing, photography, and related arts. Also presents visual-art exhibits throughout the year.

Daytona Beach Symphony Society (904) 253-2901
140 North Beach Street
P.O. Box 2
Daytona Beach, Florida 32115
Presents various touring orchestras in concert throughout the year at the Peabody Auditorium.

Daytona Playhouse (904) 255-2431
100 Jessamine Boulevard
Daytona Beach, Florida 32118-3735
Presents six plays and musicals a year.

The DeLand House Museum (904) 734-7029
137 West Michigan Avenue
DeLand, Florida 32720-3418
Headquarters of the West Volusia Historical Society. Displays furniture and artifacts from the late nineteenth and early twentieth centuries.

DeLand Museum of Art (904) 734-4371
600 North Woodland Boulevard
Deland, Florida 32730-3447
Presents rotating exhibits of work by regional artists. Annual exhibits include the Southeastern Watercolor Juried Competition and the Southeastern Fine Crafts Biennial Invitational.

Duncan Gallery of Art (904) 822-7266
Stetson University
421 North Woodland Boulevard
Deland, Florida 32720-3756
Presents a variety of visual-art exhibits throughout the year.

Enzian Theater (407)422-1725
1300 South Orlando Avenue
Maitland, Florida 32751
Presents art films throughout the year, and hosts the Florida Film Festival,
the Brouhaha Film and Video Showcase, Meet the Filmmaker programs,
workshops, and seminars.

First Street Gallery (407)321-8111
207 Magnolia Avenue
Sanford, Florida 32771
Displays artwork by local artists.

First United Methodist Church of Orlando (407)849-6080
142 East Jackson Street
Orlando, Florida 32801
Presents a wide variety of cultural offerings, both from local performers
and touring groups.

Florida Children's Repertory Theater, Inc. (407)657-4483
P.O. Box 677234
Orlando, Florida 32867
Professional company that performs for young people, primarily
in Central Florida schools.

Florida Space Coast Pops (407)632-7445
P.O. Box 3344
Cocoa, Florida 32924-3344
Presents five concerts a year, and various free performances.

Florida Symphony Youth Orchestra (407)895-3595
P.O. Box 2328
Winter Park, Florida 32790
Provides music education and performing experiences for students
of classical music.

Florida Theatrical Association (407)423-9999
201 South Orange Avenue
Orlando, Florida 32801
Presents national touring companies as part of the Orlando Broadway Series.
Also presents educational outreach programs.

Fort Christmas Historic Park (407)568-4149
1300 Fort Christmas Road
Christmas, Florida 32709
Site of the Fort Christmas replica and the Fort Christmas Museum.

Gaier Contemporary Gallery (407)897-6669
1709 North Mills Avenue
Orlando, Florida 32803-1851
Displays work by contemporary artists throughout the year.

Halifax Historical Society Museum (904)255-6976
252 South Beach Street
Daytona Beach, Florida 32114-4407
Preserves the history of the Daytona Beach area by collecting photographs,
documents, and artifacts.

Heart of the City Concerts (407)423-3441 ext. 273
First Presbyterian Church
106 East Church Street
Orlando, Florida 32801
Presents a variety of classical music and other concerts.

Holocaust Memorial and Resource Center of Central Florida
(407)628-0555
851 North Maitland Avenue
Maitland, Florida 32751
Serves as a resource for local schools. Presents art exhibits, films, theatrical
performances, and an annual arts and writing contest. Dedicated to
preserving the memory of the Holocaust.

La Maison (407)676-3111
916 East Columbus Avenue
Melbourne, Florida 32901
*An interdisciplinary art house that brings together visual arts, literary arts,
and performance arts under one roof.*

Little Theater of New Smyrna Beach (904)423-1246
726 Third Avenue
New Smyrna Beach, Florida 32168
Presents plays and musicals throughout the year.

Mad Cow Theater Company (407)599-7119
146 Orange Place
Maitland, Florida 32751
*Based at Zoe and Company in Maitland. Presents critically acclaimed plays
rarely seen elsewhere in Florida.*

Maitland Art Center (407)539-2181
231 West Packwood Avenue
Maitland, Florida 32751-5596
*Exhibits work by American artists. Housed in the historic artist compound
of André Smith.*

Maitland Historical Society and Museum (407)644-2451
P.O. Box 941001
Maitland, Florida 32794
*Preserves the history of Maitland through collections of photographs,
documents, and artifacts.*

Maitland Orchestra and Chorus (407)644-1059
620 Arapaho Trail
Maitland, Florida 32751
*Presents several pops concerts per year, including a Christmas concert
and a spring concert.*

Manhattan South Studio Theater (407)895-6557
1012 North Mills Avenue
Orlando, Florida 32803-3232
Presents theatrical performances throughout the year.

The Mark Two Dinner Theater (407)843-6275
3376 Edgewater Drive
Orlando, Florida 32804
Presents professional musical comedies and occasional plays year round.

Melbourne Civic Theater (407)723-1668
625 East New Haven Avenue
Melbourne, Florida 32901-5468
Presents a series of four to six plays and musicals a year in the
Hennegar Center.

Melbourne Municipal Band (407)724-0555
1924 Melody Land
P.O. Box 285
Melbourne, Florida 32902-0285
Presents swing, big band, pops, and classical music concerts
throughout the year.

Melon Patch Players (352)787-3013
311 North 13th Street
Leesburg, Florida 34748-4956
Present six plays and musicals a year.

Messiah Choral Society, Inc. (407)893-3288 ext. 4063
P.O. Box 3496
Winter Park, Florida 32790-3496
Performs Handel's Messiah annually in December with chorus
and orchestra.

MicheLee Puppets, Inc. (407)895-7925
P.O. Box 574704
Orlando, Florida 32857-4704
Presents puppet shows aimed at helping children develop an acceptance of
others, without regard to their abilities, disabilities, race, or ethnicity.

Mount Dora Center for the Arts (352)383-0880
138 East 5th Avenue
Mount Dora, Florida 32757-5573
Sponsers various arts and crafts exhibits throughout the year. Also offers art instruction and workshops.

Mount Dora Historical Society (352)383-5228
P.O. Box 1166
Mount Dora, Florida 32757
Active in the preservation of historic buildings and the collection of historical data.

Mount Dora Theater Company
(formerly the Icehouse Theater) (352)383-4616
1100 North Unser Street
Mount Dora, Florida 32757
Presents six plays and musicals a year, and a series of several alternative shows.

Museum of Arts and Sciences (904)255-0285
1040 Museum Boulevard
Daytona Beach, Florida 32114-4510
Displays several permanent exhibits celebrating Florida history, and rotating exhibits of visual art. The museum has an extensive permanent collection and hosts touring art exhibits.

The National Railway Historical Museum and Society, Central
Florida Chapter (407)656-8749
906 Center Street
Ocoee, Florida 34761-2325
Exhibits aimed at keeping the memory of railroads and their significance to the area alive.

OCCA, Inc. (Orlando Celebrity Concerts Association)
(407)896-2451
1900 North Mills Avenue, Suite 6
Orlando, Florida 32803
Presents the world's greatest symphony orchestras in concert locally under the name "Festival of Orchestras."

Orange County Historical Society, Inc. (407)897-6350
812 East Rollins Street
Orlando, Florida 32803
Operates the Orange County Historical Museum. Presents rotating exhibits celebrating local history.

Orlando City Ballet (407)695-4752
Royal Dance Center
1426 Tuscawilla Road #137
Winter Springs, Florida 32708
A pre-professional dance company for young people. Provides dance training and presents performances.

Orlando Concert Band, Inc. (407)678-4841
2207 Winter Woods Boulevard
Winter Park, Florida 32792-1905
Performs concerts of wind and percussion ensembles throughout the year.

Orlando Deanery Boys Choir (407)849-0680
Cathedral of St. Luke
130 North Magnolia Avenue
Orlando, Florida 32802
Presents liturgical music concerts throughout the year.

Orlando Deanery Girls Choir (407)849-0680
Cathedral of St. Luke
130 North Magnolia Avenue
Orlando, Florida 32802
Presents liturgical music concerts throughout the year.

Orlando Gay Chorus (407)645-5866
P.O. Box 3103
Orlando, Florida 32802
Presents three concerts a year. The aim of the group is to promote musical excellence and offer a positive image of gays and lesbians.

Orlando Museum of Art (407)896-4231
2416 North Mills Avenue
Orlando, Florida 32803-4314
The area's largest visual-art museum. Presents a variety of rotating exhibits, including significant national and international exhibits. Offers educational workshops and art classes.

Orlando Opera Company (407)426-1700
1111 North Orange Avenue
Orlando, Florida 32801
Presents a season of three major operas at the Bob Carr Performing Arts Center, several Second Stage productions at the Dr. Phillips Performing Arts Center, and outreach programs in local schools. Also presents concert performances by prominent opera singers.

The Orlando Philharmonic (407)647-8525
P.O. Box 540203
Orlando, Florida 32854-0203
Formerly known as Music Orlando. Presents classical music concerts throughout the year. Also accompanies performances by the Orlando Opera Company, Southern Ballet Theater, and other groups.

Orlando Public Art Program (407)246-3351
City Hall
400 South Orange Avenue
Orlando, Florida 32801
Collects and displays art in public places throughout Orlando.

Orlando Science Center (407)896-7151
810 East Rollins Street
Orlando, Florida 32802
Presents informal science education programs in natural and physical science. Operates a planetarium.

Orlando Theater Project (407)648-0077
Seminole Community College Fine Arts Theater
100 Weldon Road
Sanford, Florida 32773
Produces the annual Orlando International Fringe Festival in April, and professional theatrical performances throughout the year.

Orlando-UCF Shakespeare Festival (407)423-6905
30 South Magnolia Avenue Suite 250
Orlando, Florida 32801
Produces two Shakespeare plays every April in repertory. Also presents staged
readings and workshops.

Ormond Memorial Art Museum and Gardens (904)676-3347
78 East Granada Boulevard
Ormond Beach, Florida 32176
Presents rotating visual-art exhibits throughout the year.

Osceola Center for the Arts (407)846-6257
P.O. Box 451088
Kissimmee, Florida 34745-1088
Hosts visual-art exhibits and theatrical performances throughout the year.
Also produces an annual Latin Festival of music, art, crafts, and food.

Osceola Center Jazz Orchestra (407)846-6257
P.O. Box 451088
Kissimmee, Florida 34745-1088
Presents concerts of jazz music throughout the year.

Osceola County Historical Society Pioneer Museum
(407)396-8644
750 North Bass Road
Kissimmee, Florida 34746-6037
Maintains historic buildings in Osceola County and displays local artifacts.

Osceola Creative Arts League (407)847-1088
P.O. Box 451088
Kissimmee, Florida 34745-1088
Based at the Osceola Center for the Arts. Presents four art exhibits a year.

Osceola Players (407)847-0176 ext. 3210
P.O. Box 451088
Kissimmee, Florida 34745-1088
Based at the Osceola Center for the Arts. Produces six theatrical
productions a year.

Phoenix Theater (407)952-5717
817 East Strawbridge Avenue
Melbourne, Florida 32901-4736
Presents a series of six plays and musicals throughout the year.

Pine Castle Folk Art Center (407)855-7461
731 East Fairlane Avenue
Orlando, Florida 32809
*Preserves and maintains local historic buildings on-site. Presents the
annual Pioneer Days event with pioneer arts-and-crafts demonstrations
and a parade through Pine Castle.*

Pioneer Settlement for the Creative Arts
(904)749-2959
P.O. Box 6
Barberville, Florida 32105
*Preserves and maintains local historic buildings on-site. Presents the
annual Fall Jamboree with pioneer arts and crafts demonstrations.*

The Ritz Theater (407)321-8111
207 Magnolia Avenue
Sanford, Florida 32771
*Stages theatrical productions in the First Street Gallery until renovations
on the theater are completed.*

Royellou Museum (352)383-0006
450 Jailhouse Lane
Mount Dora, Florida 32757
*Formerly the Mount Dora town jail. Displays artifacts from
Mount Dora's past.*

R.P.M. Dance, Inc. (407)260-2883
813 First Street
Altamonte Springs, Florida 32701-3607
*Presents avant-garde and experimental dance programs at various
venues throughout the year.*

Sanford Museum (407) 330-5698
520 East First Street
Sanford, Florida 32771
*Exhibits artifacts and memorabilia celebrating the history of Sanford
and the town founder, Henry S. Sanford.*

Seaside Music Theater (904) 274-2200
1640-4 Mason Avenue
Daytona Beach, Florida 32117
*Presents a summer repertory season of five musicals at Daytona Beach
Community College, and a winter repertory season of two musicals in the
Ormond Beach Performing Arts Center. A professional company that
performs with orchestra.*

Seminole Community College Fine Arts Gallery
(407) 328-4722 ext. 3422
100 Weldon Boulevard
Sanford, Florida 32773-6199
Presents a variety of visual-art exhibits throughout the year.

Seminole Community College Fine Arts Theater
(407) 328-2040
100 Weldon Boulevard
Sanford, Florida 32773-6199
*Presents four student productions a year, and hosts various touring
productions.*

Seminole County Historical Society (407) 321-2489
300 Bush Boulevard
Sanford, Florida 32773
*Promotes historic preservation in Seminole County, and exhibits artifacts
and memorabilia in the Museum of Seminole County History.*

Seminole Symphonic Band (407) 328-4722
100 Weldon Drive
Sanford, Florida 32773-6199
Presents six to eight concerts a year at various venues.

Shoestring Theater (904)228-3777
380 South Goodwin Street
Lake Helen, Florida 32744-2803
Produces six plays and musicals a year.

Southeast Museum of Photography (904)254-4475
Daytona Beach Community College
P.O. Box 2811
Daytona Beach, Florida 32120-2811
Presents rotating exhibits of both historic and contemporary photography.

Southern Ballet Theater (407)426-1733
111 North Orange Avenue, Suite 4
Orlando, Florida 32804
*Presents three or four classical ballet and modern dance performances a
year at the Bob Carr Performing Arts Center. Also tours the region and
performs in schools.*

SsQ Theater and Repertory (407)855-5296
4624 South Rio Grande Avenue, Suite D
Orlando, Florida 32839
Produces theatrical productions with minority performers at various venues.

The Stage (407)831-9950
188 Sausalito Boulevard
Casselberry, Florida 32707-5764
Produces approximately one play a month throughout the year.

Stage Left Theater (407)895-8855
1007 Virginia Drive
Orlando, Florida 32802-2531
*Presents a variety of theatrical productions throughout the year, ranging
from alternative theater to children's productions.*

Storytellers of Brevard (407)452-6772
445 Nelson Drive
Merritt Island, Florida 32953
Presents storytelling programs throughout the year and annual
presentations of Into the Wind, a theatrical celebration of
Native American culture.

Stover Theater (904)822-8700
Stetson University
535 North Florida Avenue
Deland, Florida 32720
Produces five plays a year.

Surfside Playhouse (407)783-3127
320 South 5th Street
Cocoa Beach, Florida 32931
Produces plays and musicals throughout the year.

Theater Center (904)736-7456
600 North Woodland Boulevard
Deland, Florida 32720-3447
Located in the DeLand Cultural Arts Center. Home of the Rivertown
Players and the Storybook Theater Company. Produces plays and
musicals throughout the year.

Theater Downtown (407)841-0083
2113 North Orange Avenue
Orlando, Florida 32804
Presents a variety of theatrical performances throughout the year,
including alternative works often ignored by other theater companies.

Theater UCF (407)823-1500
University of Central Florida
4000 Central Florida Boulevard
Orlando, Florida 32817
Presents student productions throughout the year.

Theater Winter Haven (941) 299-2672
P.O. Drawer 1239
Winter Haven, Florida 32882-1230
Presents five plays per season including musicals, dramas, and comedies.

Titusville Playhouse (407) 268-1125
301 Julia Street
Titusville, Florida 32796-3520
Located in the Emma Parrish Theater. Produces six plays and musicals a year.

Troupe of Silver Stars (407) 647-3199
829 Jamestown Drive
Winter Park, Florida 32792
A theater company primarily made up of senior citizens. Presents three to four plays a year.

University of Central Florida Art Gallery
(407) 823-2676
4000 Central Florida Boulevard
Orlando, Florida 32817
Displays a variety of rotating visual-art exhibits throughout the year.

Valencia Character Company (407) 275-1603
701 North Econlockhatchee Trail
Orlando, Florida 32825-6499
Located in Orlando on VCC's east campus. Presents student theatrical productions throughout the year.

Valencia Community College Gallery (407) 299-5000
1800 South Kirkman Road
Orlando, Florida 32811-2399
Both the east and west campuses of VCC have art galleries with rotating exhibits.

Wekiva River Players (407)262-1801
P.O. Box 915271
Longwood, Florida 32791-5271
Performs a series of plays and musicals at various venues. All productions benefit local charities.

Winter Park Historical Museum and Association
(407)647-0823
P.O. Box 51
Winter Park, Florida 32790
Collects and exhibits artifacts and memorabilia from Winter Park history.

Women's Caucus for Art, Central Florida Chapter
(407)331-5008
110 West Colonial Drive
Orlando, Florida 32801
Based in Orlando. Presents several juried art shows of works by the member artists at various venues throughout the year.

Zora Neale Hurston National Museum of Fine Arts
(407)647-3307
227 East Kennedy Boulevard
Eatonville, Florida 32751-5303
Displays the creative works of Africa-descended artists from around the world throughout the year, including an annual student exhibition.

Appendix B

Central Florida Sites on the National Register of Historic Places

Orange County

Apopka Seaboard Air Line Railway Depot
36 East Station Street, Apopka
Listed 3/15/93

Brewer, Edward Hill, House
240 Trismen Terrace, Winter Park
Listed 4/22/82

Bridges, J. J., House
704 Kuhl Avenue, Orlando
Listed 1/26/84

Carroll Building
407–409 South Park Avenue, Apopka
Listed 3/4/94

Comstock-Harris House
724 Bonita Drive, Winter Park
Listed 1/13/83

Eatonville Historic District
Roughly bounded by Wymore Road, Eaton Street, Fords
Avenue, East Avenue, Ruffel Street, and Clark Street, Eatonville
Listed 2/3/98

First Church of Christ Scientist
24 North Rosalind Avenue, Orlando
Listed 6/3/80

Griffin Park Historic District
Roughly bounded by Acondale and South
Division Avenues, Carter Street and I-4, Orlando
Listed 7/18/96

Huttig, John N., Estate
435 Peachtree Road, Orlando
Listed 1/21/93

Knowles Memorial Chapel
1000 Holt Avenue
Winter Park
Listed 12/8/97

Lake Eola Historic District
Roughly bounded by Hillcrest Street, North Hyer Avenue,
Ridgewood Street, and North Magnolia Avenue, Orlando
Listed 1/16/92

Maitland Art Center
231 West Packwood Avenue, Maitland
Listed 11/17/82

Mitchill-Tibbetts House
21 East Orange Street, Apopka
Listed 11/7/91

Mizell-Leu House Historic District
1730 North Forest Avenue, Orlando
Listed 12/29/94

Ocoee Christian Church
15 South Bluford Avenue, Ocoee
Listed 3/28/97

Old Orlando Railroad Depot
Depot Place and West Church Street, Orlando
Listed 12/29/94

Palmer, Cal, Memorial Building
502 Main Street, Windermere
Listed 11/29/95

Phillips, Dr. P., House
135 Lucerne Circle NE, Orlando
Listed 7/10/79

Rogers Building
37–39 South Magnolia Avenue, Orlando
Listed 7/7/83

Ryan & Company Lumber Yard
215 East Fifth Street, Apopka
Listed 2/25/93

Tilden, Lither F., House
940 Tildenville School Road, Winter Garden
Listed 11/15/96

Tinker Building
16–18 West Pine Street, Orlando
Listed 7/17/80

Twin Mounds Archeological District
Address Restricted, Sorrento
Listed 1/19/92

Waite-Davis House
5 South Central Avenue, Apopka
Listed 8/2/90

Waterhouse, William H., House
820 South Lake Lily Drive, Maitland
Listed 2/2/83

Windermere Town Hall
520 Main Street, Windermere
Listed 6/3/94

Winter Garden Downtown Historic District
Roughly bounded by Woodland, Tremaine, Henderson,
and Lake View Streets, Winter Garden
Listed 8/1/96

Winter Garden Historic Residential District
Roughly bounded by Plant, Boyd, Tilden, and Central Streets,
Winter Garden
Listed 8/1/96

Withers-Maguire House
16 East Oakland Avenue, Ocoee
Listed 4/2/87

Woman's Club of Winter Park
419 Interlachen Avenue, Winter Park
Listed 5/4/95

Seminole County

Bradlee-McIntyre House
130 West Warren Avenue, Longwood
Listed 3/28/91

Longwood Historic District
Roughly bounded by West Pine Avenue, South Milwee Street,
Palmetto Avenue, and County Road 427, Longwood
Listed 10/5/90

Longwood Hotel
Old Dixie Highway, Longwood
Listed 5/10/84

Old Fernald-Laughton Memorial Hospital
500 South Oak Avenue, Sanford
Listed 5/21/87

Sanford Commercial District
Parts of 1st, 2nd, and Commercial Streets, between
Palmetto and Oak Streets, Sanford
Listed 6/15/76

Sanford Grammar School
7th and Myrtle Streets, Sanford
Listed 11/23/84

Sanford Residential Historic District
Roughly bounded by Sanford Avenue, 14th Street,
Elm Avenue, and 3rd Street, Sanford
Listed 12/15/89

St. James A.M.E. Church
819 Cypress Avenue, Sanford
Listed 4/24/92

Osceola County

Colonial Estate
2450 Old Dixie Highway, Kissimmee
Listed 1/3/94

Desert Inn
5570 South Kenansville Road, Yeehaw Junction
Listed 1/3/94

First United Methodist Church
215 East Church Street, Kissimmee
Listed 1/3/94

Grand Army of the Republic Memorial Hall
1101 Massachusetts Avenue, St. Cloud
Listed 2/21/97

Kissimmee Historic District
Roughly bounded by Aultman Street, Monument Avenue,
Penfield Street, and Randolph Avenue, Kissimmee
Listed 1/4/94

Old Holy Redeemer Catholic Church
120 North Spoule Avenue, Kissimmee
Listed 1/3/94

Osceola County Courthouse
Bounded by Emmett, Bryan, Rose, and Vernon Streets,
Kissimmee
Listed 8/16/77

Lake County

Bowers Bluff Middens Archeological District
Address Restricted, Astor
Listed 2/1/80

Clermont Woman's Club
655 Broome Street, Clermont
Listed 1/7/93

Clifford House
536 North Bay Street, Eustis
Listed 4/4/75

Donnelly House
Donnelly Avenue, Mount Dora
Listed 4/4/75

Duncan, Harry C., House
426 Lake Dora Drive, Tavares
Listed 8/8/97

Ferran Park and the Alice McClelland Memorial Bandshell
Ferran Park Road and Orange Avenue, Eustis
Listed 6/23/94

Holy Trinity Episcopal Church
Spring Lake Road, Fruitland Park
Listed 12/27/74

Howey House
Citrus Street, Howey in the Hills
Listed 1/27/83

Kilball Island Midden Archeological Site
Address Restricted, Astor
Listed 12/11/79

Lakeside Inn
100 North Alexander Street, Mount Dora
Listed 3/19/87

Lee School
207 North Lee Street, Leesburg
Listed 2/17/95

Mote-Morris House
1021 North Main Street, Leesburg
Listed 2/17/95

Mount Dora A.C.L. Railroad Station
341 Alexander Street, Mount Dora
Listed 3/5/92

Norton, Gould Hyde, House
1390 East Lakeview Drive, Eustis
Listed 5/16/97

Pendleton, William Kimbrough, House
1208 Chesterfield Road, Eustis
Listed 1/13/83

Taylor, Moses J., House
117 Diedrich Street, Eustis
Listed 8/1/97

Woman's Club of Eustis
227 North Center Street, Eustis
Listed 8/5/91

Volusia County

The Abbey
426 South Beach Street, Daytona Beach
Listed 4/9/87

All Saint's Episcopal Church
Corner of DeBary Avenue NE and Clark Street, Enterprise
Listed 5/13/74

Anderson, John, Lodge
71 Orchard Land, Ormond Beach
Listed 9/6/89

Anderson-Price Memorial Library Building
42 North Beach Street, Ormond Beach
Listed 1/26/84

Barberville Central High School
1776 Lightfoot Lane, Barberville
Listed 2/3/93

Bethune-Cookman College Historic District
620 Dr. Mary McLeod Bethune Boulevard, Daytona Beach
Listed 3/21/96

Bethune, Mary McLeod, Home
Bethune-Cookman College Campus, Daytona Beach
Listed 12/2/74

Blodgett, Delos A., House
404 Ridgewood Avenue, Daytona Beach
Listed 8/2/93

The Casements
15 East Granada Avenue, Ormond Beach
Listed 6/30/72

Casements Annex
127 Riverside Drive, Ormond Beach
Listed 10/6/88

Coronado Historic District
Roughly bounded by Columbus, Due East, and Pine Avenues,
and the Indian River, New Smyrna Beach
Listed 2/21/97

Cypress Street Elementary School
900 Cypress Street, Daytona Beach
Listed 12/2/96

Daytona Beach Surfside Historic District
Roughly bounded by Auditorium Boulevard, the Atlantic
Ocean, U.S. 92, and the Halifax River, Daytona Beach
Listed 8/1/96

DeBary Hall
DeBary Mansion State Park, DeBary
Listed 7/24/72

DeLand Hall
Stetson University Campus, DeLand
Listed 1/27/83

DeLand Memorial Hospital
230 North Stone Street, DeLand
Listed 11/27/89

Dickinson Memorial Library and Park
148 South Volusia Avenue, Orange City
Listed 2/8/95

Dix House
178 North Beach Street, Ormond Beach
Listed 9/6/89

Donnelly, Bartholomew J., House
801 North Peninsula Drive, Daytona Beach
Listed 8/2/93

Downtown DeLand Historic District
Roughly bounded by Florida and Rich Avenues, Woodland
Boulevard, and Howry Avenue, DeLand
Listed 12/23/87

Dunlawton Avenue Historic District
Roughly along Dunlawton Avenue to Lafayette Avenue,
Orange Avenue, and Wellman Street, Port Orange
Listed 2/5/98

Dunlawton Plantation-Sugar Mill Ruins
West of Port Orange off Nova Road, Port Orange
Listed 8/28/73

El Pino Parque Historic District
1412–1604 North Halifax Drive, Daytona
Listed 4/26/93

El Real Retiro
636 North Riverside Drive and 647 Faulkner Street,
New Smyrna Beach
Listed 11/10/87

Gamble Place Historic District
1819 Taylor Road, Port Orange
Listed 9/29/93

Grace Episcopal Church and Guild Hall
4100 Ridgewood Avenue, Port Orange
Listed 2/5/98

Halifax Drive Historic District
Roughly along Halifax Drive from Dunlawton Avenue to
Herbert Street, Port Orange
Listed 2/5/98

The Hammocks
311 John Anderson Highway, Ormond Beach
Listed 9/5/89

Haynes, Alexander, House
128 West Howry Avenue, DeLand
Listed 9/7/95

Holly Hill Municipal Building
1065 Ridgewood Avenue, Holly Hill
Listed 4/8/93

Kilkoff House
1145 West New York Avenue
DeLand
Listed 10/8/97

Kling, Amos, House
220–222 Magnolia Avenue, Daytona Beach
Listed 12/2/93

Kress, S. H., and Co. Building
140 South Beach Street, Daytona Beach
Listed 7/7/83

Lake Helen Historic District
Roughly bounded by West New York, Lakeview, Park, and
Euclid Avenues, Lake Helen
Listed 9/16/93

Lippincott Mansion
150 South Beach Street, Ormond Beach
Listed 2/21/85

Merchants Bank Building
252 South Beach Street, Daytona Beach
Listed 1/6/86

Mount Taylor
Delon Springs
Listed 10/8/97

New Smyrna Beach Historic District
Roughly bounded by Riverside Drive, U.S. 1, Ronnoc Lane,
and Smith Street, New Smyrna Beach
Listed 4/26/90

New Smyrna Beach Sugar Mill Ruins
1 mile west of New Smyrna Beach, New Smyrna Beach
Listed 8/12/70

Nocoroco
2 miles north of Ormond Beach, Ormond Beach
Listed 5/7/73

Olds Hall
340 South Ridgewood Avenue, Daytona Beach
Listed 9/23/93

Ormond Hotel
15 East Granada Boulevard, Ormond Beach
Listed 11/24/80

Ponce De Leon Inlet Lighthouse
U.S. Coast Guard Reservation, Ponce de Leon Inlet
Listed 9/22/72

The Porches
176 South Beach Street, Daytona Beach
Listed 9/11/86

Port Orange Florida East Coast Railway Freight Depot
4150 Herbert Street, Port Orange
Listed 2/5/98

Raelene
253 John Anderson Highway, Ormond Beach
Listed 10/6/88

Rogers House
436 North Beach Street, Daytona Beach
Listed 9/11/86

Ross Hammock Site
Address Restricted, Oak Hill
Listed 2/5/81

Seminole Rest
East of FL 5, western shore of Mosquito Lagoon, Canaveral
National Seashore, Oak Hill
Listed 3/19/97

Seybold Baking Company Factory
800 Orange Avenue, Daytona Beach
Listed 10/30/97

South Beach Historic District
Roughly bounded by Volusia Avenue, South Beach Street,
South Street, and U.S. 1, Daytona Beach
Listed 9/15/88

Southern Cassadaga Spiritualist Camp Historic District
Roughly bounded by Cassadaga Road and Marion, Stevens,
Lake, and Chauncy Streets, Cassadaga
Listed 3/14/91

Southwest Daytona Beach Black Heritage District
Roughly bounded by Foote Court, South Street, Dr. Martin
Luther King Boulevard, and the Florida East Coast Railroad
tracks, Daytona Beach
Listed 5/23/97

Spruce Creek Mound Complex
Address Restricted, Port Orange
Listed 12/3/90

Stetson University Campus Historic District
Roughly bounded by Michigan Avenue, North Florida
Avenue, West University Avenue, and a line south from North
Hayden Avenue, DeLand
Listed 3/14/91

Stetson, John B., House
1031 Camphor Lane, DeLand
Listed 11/21/78

Stevens, Ann, House
201 East Kicklighter Road, Lake Helen
Listed 8/18/93

Strawn Historic Agricultural District
Bounded by Broderick and Retta Streets, and by Central and
Dundee Avenues, DeLeon Springs
Listed 9/13/93

Strawn Historic Citrus-Packing House District
5707 Lake Winona Road, DeLeon Springs
Listed 9/13/93

Strawn Historic Sawmill District
5710 Lake Winona Road, DeLeon Springs
Listed 9/13/93

Talahloka
10 Orchard Lane, Ormond Beach
Listed 9/6/89

Thurman, Howard, House
614 Whitehall Street, Daytona Beach
Listed 2/23/90

Tourist Church
501 North Wild Olive Avenue, Daytona Beach
Listed 10/6/95

Turtle Mound
Address Restricted, New Smyrna Beach
Listed 9/29/70

U.S. Post Office
200 North Beach Street, Daytona Beach
Listed 9/29/70

West DeLand Residential District
Roughly bounded by University, Florida, New York, and
Orange Avenues, DeLand
Listed 11/20/92

White Hall
640 Second Avenue, Daytona Beach
Listed 7/15/92

Woman's Club of New Smyrna
403 Magnolia Avenue, New Smyrna Beach
Listed 5/11/89

Young, S. Cornelia, Memorial Library
302 Vermont Avenue, Daytona Beach
Listed 6/25/92

Brevard County

Aladdin Theater
300 Brevard Avenue, Cocoa
Listed 10/17/91

Barton Avenue Residential District
11–59 Barton Avenue, Rockledge
Listed 8/21/92

Cape Canaveral Air Force Station
Launch Pads 5, 6, 13, 14, 19, 26, and 34 and
Mission Control Center, Cocoa
Listed 4/16/84

City Point Community Church
3783 North Indian River Drive, Cocoa
Listed 6/20/95

Community Chapel of Melbourne Beach
501 Ocean Avenue, Melbourne Beach
Listed 5/14/92

Field, J. R., Homestead
750 Field Manor Drive, Indianola
Listed 9/11/97

Florida Power and Light Company Ice Plant
1604 South Harbor City Boulevard, Melbourne
Listed 11/17/82

Gleason, William H., House
1736 Pineapple Avenue, Melbourne
Listed 1/25/97

Hill, Dr. George E., House
870 Indianola Drive, Merritt Island
Listed 3/3/94

Hotel Mims
3202 State Road 46, Mims
Listed 7/28/95

Indian Fields
Address Restricted, Titusville
Listed 4/14/94

La Grange Church and Cemetery
1575 Old Dixie Highway, Titusville
Listed 12/7/95

Launch Complex 39
Kennedy Space Center, Titusville
Listed 5/24/73

Melbourne Beach Pier
Ocean Avenue and Riverside Drive, Melbourne Beach
Listed 4/12/84

Old Haulover Canal
Address Restricted, Merritt Island
Listed 12/19/78

Persimmon Mound
Address Restricted, Rockledge
Listed 4/14/94

Porcher House
434 Delannoy Avenue, Cocoa
Listed 1/6/86

Pritchard House
424 South Washington Avenue, Titusville
Listed 1/12/90

Robbins, Judge George, House
703 Indian River Avenue, Titusville
Listed 1/12/90

Rockledge Drive Residential District
15–23 Rockledge Avenue, 219–1361 Rockledge Drive,
and 1–11 Orange Avenue, Rockledge
Listed 8/21/92

Spell House
1200 Riverside Drive, Titusville
Listed 1/12/90

St. Gabriel's Episcopal Church
414 Palm Avenue, Titusville
Listed 12/5/72

St. Joseph's Catholic Church
Millwer Street NE, Palm Bay
Listed 12/3/87

St. Luke's Episcopal Church and Cemetery
5555 North Tropical Trail, Courtenay
Listed 6/15/90

Titusville Commercial District
Roughly bounded by Julia Street, Hopkins Avenue, Main
Street and Indian River Avenue, Titusville
Listed 1/10/90

Valencia Subdivision Residential District
14–140 Valencia Road, 825–827 Osceola Drive, and 24–28
Orange Avenue, Rockledge
Listed 8/21/92

Wager House
621 Indian River Avenue, Titusville
Listed 1/10/90

Whaley, Marion S., Citrus Packing House
2275 U.S. 1, Rockledge
Listed 4/8/93

Windover Archeological Site
Address Restricted, Titusville
Listed 4/20/87

Appendix C

Calendar of Annual Arts and Cultural Festivals in Central Florida

January

Zora Neale Hurston Festival of the Arts and Humanities
Features academic discussions, public forums, musical and theatrical performances, and a two-day street festival. For more information: (407)647-3307.

Scottish Highland Games
Presented by the Scottish-American Society of Central Florida. Features Scottish music, dance, food, and traditions. Held at various venues. For more information: (407)426-7268.

New Smyrna Indian River Native American Festival
Features exhibition dancing, Native American food, storytelling, and craft demonstrations. Held at the Silver Sands Arena in New Smyrna Beach. For more information: (904)424-0860.

February

Mount Dora Art Festival
A juried outdoor art festival featuring hundreds of selected artists. Held in downtown Mount Dora. For more information: (352)383-0880.

Black History Month Festival
A month-long series of events celebrating African American history at various venues throughout Central Florida. For more information: (407)290-0193.

South Asian Film Festival
Features art films from India. Presented by the Asian Cultural Association at the Enzian Theater in Maitland. For more information: (407)422-1725.

Central Florida Renaissance Festival

A recreation of a sixteenth-century village, featuring more than 100 craft shops, jousting, games, music, and period food. Held on the L & L Acres Ranch in Lake Mary-Heathrow. For more information: (407)380-9151.

Silver Spurs Rodeo

Features demonstrations of cowboy culture. Held at the Silver Spurs Arena in Kissimmee. For more information: (407)677-6336.

Winter Park Bach Festival

A music festival celebrating the works of J. S. Bach and other classical composers, featuring the 100-voice Bach Festival choir, orchestra, and soloists. Held on the campus of Rollins College in Winter Park. For more information: (407)646-2182.

March

Winter Park Bach Festival (*see above under February*)

Kissimmee Kiwanis Bluegrass Festival

Features national and local performers of bluegrass music. Held on the Silver Spurs Rodeo Grounds in Kissimmee. For more information: (800)473-7773.

Rotary Orlando International Street Painting Festival

Professional artists and art students create works with chalk and pastels on the sidewalk in front of Orlando City Hall. Includes music and dance performances. For more information: (407)649-8012.

Cocoa Village Jazz Festival

A celebration of jazz music, featuring national and local musicians. Held in downtown Cocoa. For more information: (407)459-2200.

Winter Park Sidewalk Art Festival

An outdoor juried art show featuring hundreds of selected artists. Includes musical performances. Held in downtown Winter Park. For more information: (407)672-6390.

Images Art Festival

An outdoor juried art show featuring hundreds of selected artists. Held in downtown New Smyrna Beach. For more information: (904)423-4733.

Leesburg Art Festival
An outdoor juried art show featuring hundreds of selected artists.
Held in the Venetian Gardens on Lake Harris in Leesburg.
For more information: (352)787-0000.

World Fest
An international arts, crafts, and music festival. Held in Kissimmee
Lakefront Park. For more information: (407)846-6257.

Founders Day Arts and Crafts Festival
Features hundreds of booths of arts and crafts. Proceeds benefit Historic
Preservation in Longwood. Held in the Longwood Historic District.
For more information: (407)260-3440.

Florida Irish Festival
Features Irish music, dance, food, and arts and crafts. Held at the
Seminole Greyhound Park. For more information: (407)872-7695.

Orlando-UCF Shakespeare Festival
Features two Shakespeare plays in repertory. Held at the Walt Disney
World Ampitheater in Lake Eola Park in downtown Orlando.
For more information: (407)423-6905.

April

Orlando-UCF Shakespeare Festival (see above under March)

Orlando International Fringe Festival
More than 500 performances of alternative theater and music.
Held at various venues in downtown Orlando. For more information:
(407)648-0077.

DeLand Outdoor Art Festival
An outdoor juried art show featuring hundreds of selected artists.
Held at Earl Brown Park in DeLand. For more information:
(904)734-8333.

Maitland Spring Arts and Crafts Show
Featuring hundreds of booths of arts and crafts. Held on Lake Lily in
Maitland. For more information: (407)644-0741.

Melbourne Art Festival
An outdoor juried art show featuring hundreds of selected artists. Held in historic downtown Melbourne. For more information: (407)722-1964.

Jazz Fest Kissimmee
A music festival featuring international and local jazz artists. Held in Kissimmee Lakefront Park. For more information: (407)846-6257.

Fiesta Medina
A celebration of Latin culture, featuring music, food, and dance. Held in Orlando Festival Park. For more information: (407)381-5310.

Latin Fiesta
A two-day festival celebrating Hispanic culture. Features food, music, dance, and crafts. Held at Lake Eola Park in downtown Orlando. For more information: (407)657-9172.

Cracker Day
Features country music, food, dance, and competitions. Held at the Cattlemen's Arena in DeLand. For more information: (407)330-5150.

Storytelling Fest
A two-day gathering of storytellers presented by the Florida Storytelling Guild. Held at the Stephen Foster State Folk Culture Center in White Springs. For more information: (904)397-4331.

Spring Fiesta in the Park
A juried arts and crafts show with about 175 artisans. Held at Lake Eola Park in downtown Orlando. For more information: (407)422-7649.

Art in the Park
A small outdoor arts and crafts show. Held at Donnelly Park in downtown Mount Dora. For more information: (352)735-1191.

May

Orlando-UCF Shakespeare Festival (*see above under March*)

Central Florida Dance Festival
Features as many as fifteen local dance studios performing ballet, modern, jazz, ballroom, musical theater, and ethnic dance. Held in the Walt

Disney World Amphitheater at Lake Eola Park in downtown Orlando. For more information: (407)695-4752.

Up, Up, and Away
Juried fine arts show featuring hundreds of artists. Held in the Orlando International Airport. For more information: (407)825-3885.

A Taste of Oviedo
Features food from area restaurants, an arts and crafts show, and musical performances. Held in downtown Oviedo. For more information: (407)365-6500.

June

Florida Film Festival
Celebrates film as art. More than 100 films including features, documentaries, and shorts are presented. Seminars, special guests, a student competition, and an awards banquet are also featured. Held at the Enzian Theater in Maitland and other Central Florida venues. For more information: (407)629-1088.

July

Florida International Festival
Presented in odd-numbered years. Features a series of concerts by the London Symphony Orchestra and internationally known soloists as well as dance, theatrical, and other musical performances. Held at various venues in Daytona Beach. For more information: (904)252-1511.

International Guitar Workshop
Features seminars, master classes, and public performances by international and local classical guitarists. Held at Stetson University in DeLand. For more information: (904)734-1087.

August

Florida International Festival (see above under July)

Fine Art and Jazz Show
Features performances by local jazz bands, fine art displays, and wine tastings. Held at the Lakeridge Winery and Vineyards in Clermont. For more information: (904)394-8627.

September

Osceola Art Festival
An outdoor arts and crafts festival featuring hundreds of artists. Held in Kissimmee Lakefront Park. For more information: (407)931-1646.

Mexican Independence Day Festival
A celebration recognizing the independence of Mexico presented by the Mexican Consulate in Orlando. Features Mexican music, food, dance, and crafts. Held at Lake Eola Park in downtown Orlando. For more information: (407)894-0514.

October

Winter Park Autumn Art Festival
Presented by the Cornell Fine Arts Museum and the Crealde School of Art. Features work by hundreds of Florida artists. Held on the campus of Rollins College in Winter Park. For more information: (407)646-2526.

Viva Osceola Festival
Presented by the Osceola Center for the Arts. Features Latin music, food, dance, art, and crafts. Held at Kissimmee Lakefront Park. For more information: (407)846-6257.

Lake Mary-Heathrow Festival of the Arts
An outdoor art festival featuring works by hundreds of artists. Held at the L & L Acres Ranch in Lake Mary. For more information: (407)333-2357.

Cocoa Village Fall Craft Show
An outdoor show featuring hundreds of booths of arts and crafts. Held in Cocoa Village. For more information: (407)631-9075.

Maitland Art Festival
An outdoor juried show featuring hundreds of artists. Held in Maitland. For more information: (407)263-5218.

Pioneer Days Festival
Features demonstrations of pioneer lifestyles and crafts. Held on South Orange Avenue in Pine Castle. For more information: (407)855-7461.

Halifax Art Festival
An outdoor art festival featuring hundreds of artists. Held on the campus of Daytona Beach Community College. For more information: (904)788-4718.

Seminole Indian and Florida Pioneer Festival
Features demonstrations and exhibitions focusing on Native American and pioneer culture. Held on the Cocoa campus of Brevard Community College. For more information: (407)632-1111.

Downtown Melbourne Fall Art and Craft Festival
An outdoor art festival held in Melbourne's historic district. For more information: (407)724-1741.

November

Festival of the Masters
An outdoor art festival featuring work by hundreds of artists from around the world. Held at the Disney Village Marketplace in Lake Buena Vista. For more information: (407)824-4321.

DeLand Fall Festival of the Arts
A juried outdoor art festival featuring work by hundreds of artists. Held in the DeLand Historic District. For more information: (904)734-4371.

Barberville Fall Jamboree
Features historical displays, demonstrations of pioneer arts and crafts, cooking, dance, music, and storytelling. Held at the Barberville Pioneer Settlement for the Creative Arts. For more information: (904)749-2959.

Celebration of Old Daytona
Presented by the Old Daytona Civic Association. Features tours of Daytona's historic homes and sites, Civil War reenactments, and musical performances. Held in downtown Daytona. For more information: (904)255-6976.

American Indian Cultural Festival
Features craft demonstrations, food, and intertribal dancing. Held at City Island Park in Daytona Beach. For more information: (904)253-3827.

Longwood Arts and Crafts Festival
A fund-raiser for the Central Florida Society for Historic Preservation.
Features hundreds of booths of arts and crafts. Held in Longwood's
Historic District. For more information: (407)332-6920.

Fiesta in the Park
One of the largest outdoor arts and crafts shows in Central Florida,
featuring more than 500 booths. Held at Lake Eola Park in downtown
Orlando. For more information: (407)422-7649.

December

Winter Springs Art Festival
An outdoor art festival featuring works by hundreds of selected artists.
Held at Central Winds Park in Winter Springs. For more information:
(407)682-7570.

A Latin Christmas Celebration
Presentations of Latin Christmas traditions, including music, drama,
dance, and food. Held at the Osceola Center for the Arts in Kissimmee.
For more information: (407)846-6257.

Kwanzaa Festival
A festival celebrating the African American tradition of Kwanzaa.
Featuring poetry readings, storytelling, music, dance, and seminars.
Held at various venues throughout Central Florida.
For more information: (407)290-6751.

Native American Indian Festival
Celebrates the heritage of Native Americans. Held at the Melbourne
campus of Brevard Community College. For more information:
(407)253-6149.

Cracker Christmas
Features pioneer-style arts and crafts. Held at Fort Christmas Historical
Park. For more information: (407)568-4149.

Florida Living History Festival
Features displays celebrating Florida history and pioneer craft demonstrations. Held at the Casements in Ormond Beach. For more information:
(904)676-3216.

Notes

Introduction

1. Interview with Maya Angelou, January 1994.
2. Interview with Marena Grant Morrisey, April 1997.
3. Interview with Glenda Hood, March 1996.
4. Ecotourism/Heritage Tourism Advisory Committee, "Plan" (working draft).
5. Interview with Sara Van Arsdel, February 1996.

Orlando

1. Kendrick, *Orlando: A Century Plus*, 119–21.
2. Robison and Andrews, *Flashbacks*, 268.
3. Bacon, *Orlando: A Centennial History*, 2:265.
4. Kendrick, *Orlando: A Century Plus*, 121.
5. Kendrick, *Orlando: A Century Plus*, 121–22.
6. Robison and Andrews, *Flashbacks*, 273.
7. Robison and Andrews, *Flashbacks*, 259.
8. Kendrick, *Orlando: A Century Plus*, 1.
9. Kendrick, *Orlando: A Century Plus*, 38.
10. Spear, "Picking Up the Past," *Orlando Sentinel*, July 19, 1997.
11. Bacon, *Orlando: A Centennial History*, 1:59.
12. Kendrick, *Orlando: A Century Plus*, 5.
13. Bacon, *Orlando: A Centennial History*, 1:14.
14. Bacon, *Orlando: A Centennial History*, 1:14.
15. Fries, *Orlando in the Long, Long Ago . . . and Now*, 3–5.
16. Kendrick, *Orlando: A Century Plus*, 2.
17. Kendrick, *Orlando: A Century Plus*, 3.
18. Kendrick, *Orlando: A Century Plus*, 3–4.
19. Interview with Sara Van Arsdel, February 1996.
20. Kendrick, *Orlando: A Century Plus*, 33–35.
21. Bacon, *Orlando: A Centennial History*, 1:100.
22. Kendrick, *Orlando: A Century Plus*, 108.
23. Kendrick, *Orlando: A Century Plus*, 109.
24. Robison and Andrews, *Flashbacks*, 251.

25. Robison and Andrews, Flashbacks, 194.
26. Winsberg, *Florida's History through Its Places*, 59–60.
27. Interview with Jodi Rubin, February 1996.
28. Bacon, *Orlando: A Centennial History*, 1:284.
29. Robison and Andrews, Flashbacks, 192.
30. Interview with Geraldine Thompson, February 1996.
31. Interview with Geraldine Thompson, February 1996.
32. Interview with Geraldine Thompson, February 1996.
33. McCarthy, *Black Florida*, 222–23.
34. McCarthy, *Black Florida*, 223–24.
35. Gannon, *Florida: A Short History*, 30.
36. Brown, *Florida's First People*, 4.
37. Panagopoulos, *New Smyrna*, 20.
38. Population estimates provided by Mexican Consulate in Orlando.
39. Interview with Rene Plasencia, October 1995.
40. Interview with Rene Plasencia, October 1995.

Winter Park

1. From a list commissioned by the Avis Car Rental Company.
2. MacDowell, *Chronological History of Winter Park*, 9.
3. Campen, *Winter Park Portrait*, 9.
4. Campen, *Winter Park Portrait*, 13–14.
5. MacDowell, *Chronological History of Winter Park*, 29–32.
6. Campen, *Winter Park Portrait*, 33–36.
7. MacDowell, *Chronological History of Winter Park*, 36.
8. Otey, *Eatonville, Florida: A Brief History*, 1.
9. Campen, *Winter Park Portrait*, 21.
10. Campen, *Winter Park Portrait*, 23.
11. Campen, *Winter Park Portrait*, 31–33.
12. Sherwood, *Carving His Own Destiny*, 157.
13. Interview with Laurie Lyall, March 1997.
14. Interview with Dennis Davis, March 1995.
15. Interview with Ted Jaslow, March 1994.
16. MacDowell, *Chronological History of Winter Park*, 255.
17. Campen, *Winter Park Portrait*, 54–57.
18. Anderson, *Louis Comfort Tiffany Remembered* (television documentary).
19. Anderson, *Louis Comfort Tiffany Remembered* (television documentary).
20. Campen, *Winter Park Portrait*, 59.
21. Interview with John Tiedtke, February 1995.
22. Interview with John Tiedtke, February 1995.
23. Interview with Arthur Blumenthal, October 1995.

Eatonville

1. Nathiri, *Zora Neale Hurston: A Woman and Her Community*, 3–5.
2. Interview with N.Y. Nathiri, August 1994.
3. Otey, *Eatonville, Florida: A Brief History*, 1.
4. Otey, *Eatonville, Florida: A Brief History*, 31.
5. Hemenway, *Zora Neale Hurston: A Literary Biography*, 13.
6. Hemenway, *Zora Neale Hurston: A Literary Biography*, 11–12.
7. Hemenway, *Zora Neale Hurston: A Literary Biography*, 14.
8. Hemenway, *Zora Neale Hurston: A Literary Biography*, 19–20.
9. Hemenway, *Zora Neale Hurston: A Literary Biography*, 62–63.
10. Hemenway, *Zora Neale Hurston: A Literary Biography*, 227–30.
11. Hemenway, *Zora Neale Hurston: A Literary Biography*, 43–44.
12. Nathiri, *Zora Neale Hurston: A Woman and Her Community*, 131–34.
13. Interview with N.Y. Nathiri, January 1993.
14. From Alice Walker's "Zora Neale Hurston Festival Address," recorded by Ben Brotemarkle, January 1990.
15. Interview with Ruby Dee, January 1990.
16. Hemenway, *Zora Neale Hurston: A Literary Biography*, 334.
17. Interview with Dorothy Porter Wesley, January 1992.
18. Interview with Oscar Brown, Jr., January 1992.
19. Interview with Elizabeth Van Dyke, January 1993.
20. Interview with George C. Wolfe, January 1994.
21. Interview with George C. Wolfe, January 1994.
22. Interview with Glenda Dickerson, January 1994.
23. Interview with David E. Wharton, January 1991.
24. McCarthy, *Black Florida*, 93.
25. Interview with N.Y. Nathiri, August 1994.

Maitland

1. Hanna, *Fort Maitland*, 7–8.
2. Hanna, *Fort Maitland*, 42.
3. Robison and Andrews, *Flashbacks*, 57–58.
4. Winsberg, *Florida's History through Its Places*, 59.
5. Otey, *Eatonville, Florida: A Brief History*, 2–3
6. Nathiri, *Zora Neale Hurston: A Woman and Her Community*, 102.
7. Biographical information on André Smith provided by Maitland Art Museum.
8. Interview with Gerry Shepp, March 1995.
9. Campen, *Winter Park Portrait*, 64–65.
10. Interview with Gerry Shepp, March 1995.
11. Interview with Gerry Shepp, March 1995.

12. Winsberg, *Florida's History through Its Places*, 59.

13. Bloomgarden, *Chichen Itza*, 20.

14. Interview with Gerry Shepp, March 1995.

15. Interview with Gerry Shepp, March 1995.

16. Winsberg, *Florida's History through Its Places*, 59.

17. Interview with Siegrid Tiedtke, June 1994.

18. Interview with Oliver Stone, May 1993.

19. Interview with Philip Tiedtke, June 1992.

20. Interview with Robert Wise, April 1993.

Christmas

1. Wright, *Creeks and Seminoles*, 202.

2. Robison and Andrews, *Flashbacks*, 15.

3. Porter, *The Negro on the American Frontier*, 262.

4. Robison and Andrews, *Flashbacks*, 15

5. Wright, *Creeks and Seminoles*, 233–37, 243.

6. Wright, *Creeks and Seminoles*, 250, 258.

7. Robison and Andrews, *Flashbacks*, 23.

8. Robison and Andrews, *Flashbacks*, 245.

9. Interview with Vicky Prewett, August 1995.

10. Interview with Vicky Prewett, August 1995.

11. Wright, *Creeks and Seminoles*, 263–64.

12. Interview with Vicky Prewett, August 1995.

13. Interview with Vicky Prewett, August 1995.

14. Interview with Vicky Prewett, August 1995.

15. Interview with Trudy Trask, August 1995.

Longwood

1. Francke, *Early Days of Seminole County, Florida*, 6, 21.

2. Robison and Andrews, *Flashbacks*, 86.

3. Francke, *Early Days of Seminole County, Florida*, 21.

4. Robison and Andrews, *Flashbacks*, 86.

5. Robison and Andrews, *Flashbacks*, 177.

6. Interview with John Bistline, March 1997.

7. Parry, *Full Steam Ahead! The Story of Peter Demens*, 7–8.

8. Parry, *Full Steam Ahead! The Story of Peter Demens*, 9.

9. Parry, *Full Steam Ahead! The Story of Peter Demens*, 11.

10. Parry, *Full Steam Ahead! The Story of Peter Demens*, 14–15.

11. Parry, *Full Steam Ahead! The Story of Peter Demens*, 26.

12. Francke, *Early Days of Seminole County, Florida,* 23.

13. Interview with John Bistline, March 1997.

14. Robison and Andrews, *Flashbacks,* 214.

15. Robison and Andrews, *Flashbacks,* 187–88.

16. Francke, *Early Days of Seminole County, Florida,* 23.

17. Interview with John Bistline, March 1997.

18. Robison and Andrews, *Flashbacks,* 83.

19. Winsberg, *Florida's History through Its Places,* 81.

20. Robison and Andrews, *Flashbacks,* 188.

21. Winsberg, *Florida's History through Its Places,* 81.

22. Interview with John Bistline, March 1997.

23. Interview with Nelda Pryor, March 1997.

Sanford

1. Robison and Andrews, *Flashbacks,* 29–30.

2. Robison and Andrews, *Flashbacks,* 72.

3. Interview with Alicia Clark, April 1996.

4. Robison and Andrews, *Flashbacks,* 72–73.

5. Interview with Alicia Clark, April 1996.

6. Robison and Andrews, *Flashbacks,* 75.

7. Schaal, *Sanford As I Knew It, 1912–1935,* 7.

8. Robison and Andrews, *Flashbacks,* 182.

9. Schaal, *Sanford As I Knew It, 1912–1935,* 56.

10. Schaal, *Sanford As I Knew It, 1912–1935,* 63–67.

11. Robison and Andrews, *Flashbacks,* 251–52.

12. Interview with Alicia Clark, April 1996.

13. Winsberg, *Florida's History through Its Places,* 81.

14. Interview with Alicia Clark, April 1996.

15. Interview with Fred Rogers, May 1996.

16. Interview with Kay Bartholomew, May 1996.

17. Interview with Karen Ratliff-McNeil, April 1996.

Kissimmee

1. Cody and Cody, *Osceola County: The First 100 Years,* 114–15.

2. Akerman, *Florida Cowman,* 1–2.

3. Cody and Cody, *Osceola County: The First 100 Years,* 31.

4. Osceola County, *The Osceola County Centennial Book,* 38.

5. Hurston, "Lawrence of the River," 18, 55–57.

6. Cody and Cody, *Osceola County: The First 100 Years,* 32.

7. Cody and Cody, *Osceola County: The First 100 Years*, 41.
8. Osceola County, *The Osceola County Centennial Book*, 418–19.
9. Interview with David Snedeker, April 1997.
10. Ammer, *The Harper-Collins Dictionary of Music.* 44.
11. Interview with David Snedeker, April 1997.
12. Osceola County, *The Osceola County Centennial Book*, 24–25.
13. Osceola County, *The Osceola County Centennial Book*, 59.
14. Interview with Peter Edwards, October 1994.
15. Interview with Angie del Riego Maloney, October 1994.
16. Interview with Angie del Riego Maloney, October 1994.
17. Interview with Angie del Riego Maloney, October 1995.

Mount Dora

1. Interview with David Phelps, November 1995.
2. Longstreet, *Story of Mount Dora, Florida*, 19–21.
3. Interview with David Phelps, November 1995.
4. Longstreet, *Story of Mount Dora, Florida*, 17–18.
5. Longstreet, *Story of Mount Dora, Florida*, 19.
6. Edgerton, *Memories of Mount Dora and Lake County*, 84–86.
7. Interview with Bill West, November 1995.
8. Interview with Bill West, November 1995.
9. Edgerton, *Memories of Mount Dora and Lake County*, 108–11.
10. Interview with David Phelps, November 1995.

DeLand

1. Interview with Sallee Hardy, May 1996.
2. Francke, Gillingham, and Turner, *Volusia: The West Side*, 239–42.
3. Interview with Van Rhodes, May 1996.
4. *Souvenir of the City of DeLand, Florida*, 39–40.
5. Francke, Gillingham, and Turner, *Volusia: The West Side*, 266–68.
6. Francke, Gillingham, and Turner, *Volusia: The West Side*, 276.
7. McPhee, *Oranges*, 15.
8. Francke, Gillingham, and Turner, *Volusia: The West Side*, 332.
9. Interview with Van Rhodes, May 1996.
10. Interview with Michael Sanden, September 1995.

Cassadaga

1. Interview with Jim Watson, November 1995.
2. Interview with Kristin Congdon, November 1995.

3. Francke, Gillingham, and Turner, *Volusia: The West Side*, 230.

4. Karcher and Hutchinson, *This Way to Cassadaga*, 37–38.

5. Interview with Jim Watson, November 1995.

6. Interview with Gary Monroe, November 1995.

7. Henderson, *The Story of Cassadaga*, 11.

8. Henderson, *The Story of Cassadaga*, 12–13.

9. Henderson, *The Story of Cassadaga*, 13–14.

10. Henderson, *The Story of Cassadaga*, 14–16.

11. Francke, Gillingham, and Turner, *Volusia: The West Side*, 229–30.

12. Henderson, *The Story of Cassadaga*, 1.

13. Henderson, *The Story of Cassadaga*, 1–10.

14. Karcher and Hutchinson, *This Way to Cassadaga*, 41–42.

Barberville

1. Francke, Gillingham, and Turner, *Volusia: The West Side*, 154–56.

2. Francke, Gillingham, and Turner, *Volusia: The West Side*, 174.

3. Interview with Harold D. Cardwell, Sr., April 1997.

4. Pioneer Settlement for the Creative Arts, *Settlement Times*, 6.

5. Francke, Gillingham, and Turner, *Volusia: The West Side*, 168–69.

6. Interview with Marilyn Breeze, April 1997.

7. Francke, Gillingham, and Turner, *Volusia: The West Side*, 171.

8. Interview with Marilyn Breeze, April 1997.

9. Francke, Gillingham, and Turner, *Volusia: The West Side*, 182–83.

10. Interview with John Jerico, April 1997.

11. Interview with Harold D. Cardwell, Sr., April 1997.

Daytona Beach

1. Schene, *Hopes, Dreams, and Promises: A History of Volusia County, Florida*, 109.

2. Information provided by the Halifax Historical Society.

3. Information provided by the Halifax Historical Society.

4. Clarida, *Charles Grover Burgoyne*, 5–6.

5. Clarida, *Charles Grover Burgoyne*, 8.

6. Clarida, *Charles Grover Burgoyne*, 8–18.

7. Interview with Gary Libby, May 1997.

8. Interview with Vinton Fisher, November 1995.

9. McCarthy, *Black Florida*, 73–77.

10. Interview with Joseph Taylor, July 1997.

11. Interview with Joseph Taylor, July 1997.

12. Interview with Joseph Taylor, July 1997.

13. Interview with Tippen Davidson, July 1993.

14. Interview with Tippen Davidson, July 1993.
15. Interview with Sharron Mock, July 1995.
16. Interview with Sharron Mock, July 1995.
17. Interview with Mstislav Rostropovich, July 1991.
18. Interview with Clive Gillanson, July 1995.
19. Interview with Richard McNichol conducted by Robert B. Peterson, III, July 1995.
20. Interview with John Lawley, July 1995.
21. Interview with Tippen Davidson, July 1993.
22. Interview with Tippen Davidson, July 1993.

New Smyrna Beach

1. Panagopoulos, *New Smyrna*, 9–20.
2. Panagopoulos, *New Smyrna*, 54.
3. Panagopoulos, *New Smyrna*, 88–91.
4. Panagopoulos, *New Smyrna*, 149–52.
5. Panagopoulos, *New Smyrna*, 174–75.
6. Panagopoulos, *New Smyrna*, 188–89.
7. Winsberg, *Florida's History through Its Places*, 84.
8. Interview with Doris Leeper, September 1995.
9. Interview with Doris Leeper, September 1995.
10. Interview with Suzanne Fetcher, May 1995.
11. Interview with Edward Albee, February 1997.
12. Interview with Sonia Sanchez, May 1995.
13. Interview with Sonia Sanchez, May 1995.
14. Interview with Chinary Ung, May 1995.
15. Interview with Chinary Ung, May 1995.
16. Interview with Chinary Ung, May 1995.
17. Interview with Diane Di Prima, May 1994.
18. Interview with Bebe Moore Campbell, May 1994.
19. Interview with Jack Gelber, May 1994.
20. Interview with Jack Gelber, May 1994.
21. Interview with Suzanne Fetcher, May 1995.
22. Interview with Charles Rose, May 1995.
23. Interview with Charles Rose, May 1995.
24. Interview with Doris Leeper, September 1995.
25. Interview with Doris Leeper, September 1995.

The Space Coast

1. Rabac, *The City of Cocoa Beach: The First Sixty Years*, vi.
2. Interview with Gail Ryan, October 1995.
3. Interview with Kenneth Omi, October 1995.
4. Interview with Kenneth Omi, October 1995.
5. Rabac, *The City of Cocoa Beach: The First Sixty Years*, vi.
6. McCarthy, *Black Florida*, 54.
7. Interview with Jeff Simpson, March 1995.
8. Rabac, *The City of Cocoa Beach: The First Sixty Years*, 20–23.
9. Rabac, *The City of Cocoa Beach: The First Sixty Years*, 33, 53.
10. Crepeau, *Melbourne Village: The First Twenty-Five Years*, 127.
11. Interview with Kay Elliot Burke, December 1995.
12. Interview with Kay Elliot Burke, December 1995.
13. Interview with Christopher Confessore, November 1995.
14. Interview with Candler Schaffer, November 1995.
15. Interview with Dave Pignanelli, January 1996.

Conclusion

1. Ecotourism/Heritage Tourism Advisory Committee, "Plan" (working draft).
2. Interview with N. Y. Nathiri, August 1994.
3. Interview with Gary Libby, May 1997.
4. Interview with Glenda Hood, March 1996.
5. Interview with Sara Van Arsdel, February 1996.

Bibliography

Akerman, Joe A. *Florida Cowman: A History of Florida Cattle Raising.* Kissimmee, Fla.: Florida Cattlemen's Association, 1976.

Ammer, Christine. *The Harper-Collins Dictionary of Music.* New York: Harper-Collins, 1987.

Bacon, Eve. *Orlando: A Centennial History.* 2 vols. Chuluota, Fla.: Mickler House Publishers, 1975–77.

Bloomgarden, Richard. *The Easy Guide to Chichen Itza.* Shawnee Mission, Kansas: Forsyth Travel Library, 1987.

Brown, Robin C. *Florida's First People.* Sarasota, Fla.: Pineapple Press, 1994.

Campen, Richard N. *Winter Park Portrait: The Story of Winter Park and Rollins College.* Beachwood, Ohio: West Summit Press, 1987.

Clarida, Vince. *Charles Grover Burgoyne: The Man Who Brought Tourism to Daytona.* Daytona Beach, Fla.: Halifax Historical Society, 1997.

Cody, Aldus M., and Robert S. Cody. *Osceola County: The First 100 Years.* Kissimmee, Fla.: Osceola County Historical Society, 1987.

Crepeau, Richard C. *Melbourne Village: The First Twenty-Five Years, 1946–1971.* Orlando, Fla.: University of Central Florida Press, 1988.

Ecotourism/Heritage Tourism Advisory Committee. "Plan." Working Draft. Tallahassee, Fla.: Ecotourism/Heritage Tourism Advisory Committee, 1997.

Edgerton, David. *Memories of Mount Dora and Lake County, 1845 to 1981.* Mount Dora, Fla.: David Edgerton, 1982.

Francke, Arthur E., Jr. *Early Days of Seminole County, Florida.* Sanford, Fla.: Seminole County Historical Commission, 1995.

Francke, Arthur E., Jr., Alyce Hockaday Gillingham, and Maxine Carey Turner. *Volusia: The West Side.* DeLand, Fla.: West Volusia Historical Society, 1986.

Fries, Kena. *Orlando in the Long, Long Ago . . . and Now.* Orlando, Fla.: Ty Cobb's Florida Press, 1938.

Gannon, Michael. *Florida: A Short History.* Gainesville, Fla.: University Press of Florida, 1993.

Hanna, Alfred J. *Fort Maitland.* Maitland, Fla.: Fort Maitland Committee, 1936.

Hemenway, Robert E. *Zora Neale Hurston: A Literary Biography.* Chicago: University of Illinois Press, 1977.

Henderson, Janie. *The Story of Cassadaga.* Orlando, Fla.: Pisces Publishing, 1996.

Hurston, Zora Neale. "Lawrence of the River." *Saturday Evening Post.* September 5, 1942.

Karcher, Janet, and John Hutchinson. *This Way to Cassadaga*. Deltona, Fla.: John Hutchinson Productions, 1980.

Kendrick, Baynard H. *Orlando: A Century Plus*. Orlando, Fla.: Sentinel Star Company, 1976.

Longstreet, R. J. *The Story of Mount Dora, Florida*. Mount Dora, Fla.: Mount Dora Historical Society, 1960.

MacDowell, Claire Leavitt. *Chronological History of Winter Park, Florida*. Winter Park, Fla.: Orange Press, 1950.

McCarthy, Kevin M. *Black Florida*. New York: Hippocrene Books, 1995.

McDowell, Edwin. "Tourists Respond to Lure of Culture: Word Spreads That Art Sells." *New York Times*. April 24, 1997.

McPhee, John. *Oranges*. New York: Farrar, Strauss, and Giroux, 1984.

Nathiri, N. Y., ed. *Zora! Zora Neale Hurston: A Woman and Her Community*. Orlando, Fla.: Sentinel Books, 1991.

Osceola County. *The Osceola County Centennial Book*. Kissimmee, Fla.: Osceola County, 1987.

Otey, Frank M. *Eatonville, Florida: A Brief History*. Winter Park, Fla.: Four-G Publishers, 1989.

Panagopoulos, E. P. *New Smyrna: An Eighteenth-Century Greek Odyssey*. Gainesville, Fla.: University Press of Florida, 1966.

Parry, Albert. *Full Steam Ahead! The Story of Peter Demens*. St. Petersburg, Fla.: Great Outdoors Publishing Co., 1987.

Pioneer Settlement for the Creative Arts. *Settlement Times*. Barberville, Fla.: Pioneer Settlement for the Creative Arts, November 1996.

Porter, Kenneth Wiggins. *The Negro on the American Frontier*. New York: Arno Press, 1971.

Rabac, Glenn. *The City of Cocoa Beach: The First Sixty Years*. Winona, Minnesota: Apollo Books, 1986.

Robison, Jim, and Mark Andrews. *Flashbacks: The Story of Central Florida's Past*. Orlando, Fla.: The Orange County Historical Society, 1995.

Schaal, Peter. *Sanford As I Knew It, 1912–1935*. Orlando, Fla.: Peter Schaal, 1970.

———. *Sanford and the World War II Years, 1936–1945*. Orlando, Fla.: Peter Schaal, 1975.

Schene, Michael G. *Hopes, Dreams, and Promises: A History of Volusia County, Florida*. Daytona Beach, Fla.: News Journal Corporation, 1976.

Sherwood, Ruth. *Carving His Own Destiny: The Story of Albin Polášek*. Chicago: Ralph Fletcher Seymour Publisher, 1954.

A Souvenir of the City of DeLand, Florida. DeLand, Fla.: News Publishing Co., 1902.

Spear, Kevin. "Picking Up the Past: Radar May Have Found Fort Gatlin." *Orlando Sentinel*. July 19, 1997.

Winsberg, Morton D. *Florida's History through Its Places*. Tallahassee, Fla.: Institute of Science and Public Affairs, 1988.

Wright, J. Leitch, Jr. *Creeks and Seminoles*. Lincoln, Nebraska: University of Nebraska Press, 1986.

Index